The Heart of the Canoe

Story, Ceremony, and the Transformation of Suffering

Chris Weaver

Artwork by
Paula Nelson

Springbranch Press
Asheville, North Carolina, USA
springbranchpress.org

Springbranch Press
Asheville, North Carolina, USA
springbranchpress.org

ISBN-10:
0692784934

ISBN-13:
978-0692784938

Cover design & photo by the author

for
the world's child

Contents

Author's Preface

This is the story of a journey. Like the sound of water, it bears the echoes of many other journeys, remembered and unremembered, told and untold, weaving together.

It begins as a teacher's story. I started writing it this past summer, intending it as part of a larger book that shares a vision for a new kind of school, entitled *Living School Design & Practice*. But almost immediately, *The Heart of the Canoe* took on a life of its own. The other book had to wait as this story ran its course, like an arroyo in flash-flood after a summer thunderstorm, full of power and anguish.

In its essence, this book is an *honor song* to one girl, whom I call *the world's child*. You will meet her in these pages, at age twelve, that liminal moment between childhood and adulthood. She is not the only character in the story, but she is the power behind and between the words.

The book recounts an unlikely paddling journey I took with a class of twenty-eight fifth- and sixth-graders in June of 1999. But the inner journey of insight, challenge, and awakening continues, far beyond the paddle-strokes of our physical trip. Our starting-point was an urban public school classroom in West Seattle, and, as we understood it at the time, our destination was a gravel beach on the Suquamish Indian Reservation.

The Heart of the Canoe is thus also the story of a journey *into* Native North America. My own body does not bear the blood to tell a story *of* Native North America. My ancestors are German-Americans who lived for ten generations in the valleys of the southern Appalachians, to which the story returns before the end. But the tradition and cultural revival of the indigenous Canoe Nations of the Northwest Coast of North America form the context of this story, translated through the heart and mind of a non-Indian educator. It is appropriate that matters of Indian tradition, thus translated, be greeted with skepticism.

With this in mind, I cannot share such a story without first addressing the larger history, and speaking to the present historical moment.

It is widely accepted that from the day that Europeans first anchored their ships off the shores of this continent, the colonization of North America unfolded in great dark waves of exploitation, violence,

injustice, greed, and willful ignorance. This wide acceptance does not connote a deep or authentic understanding among non-Indians of the reality of this violence ~ its effects on Native people, its desecration of
the living land (along with the land's spiritual ties to
its indigenous ancestors), and the ways in which the
violence continues to the present day. Members of
the dominant culture (myself included) do not truly
understand these fundamental realities of intergener-
ational Indian experience.

     I know that *The Heart of the Canoe* will be read
by both Native and non-Native readers. To imagine
that their perspectives are the same is to assume an
illusory unity. Any authentic unity can only grow
from an acknowledgement of our differences and our
history. Because I know the perspectives to be vastly
different, I choose here to address these groups of
readers separately.

To Indian readers of this book:

     As a teacher of Indian and Alaska Native stu-
dents, I had the blessing of working with a number of
carvers, cultural artists, and community leaders of
the First Nations around the *Salish Sea*, who helped
us and supported us in our paddling journey in 1999.
I share my deep gratitude to these helpers now.
Most of them are named in the book. I hope that my

references to these people, and to the history and traditions of the Canoe Nations, are respectful and accurate. I am grateful to David Neel of the Fort Rupert Kwagiutl Nation in British Columbia for his remarkable book of interviews entitled *The Great Canoes*, from which I have drawn both inspiration and information to support the telling of this story. I ask forgiveness for any errors I may have made, and invite feedback and correction from readers (as I can easily make changes for future printings).

As a teacher who has devoted my life to culture change in the realm of education, I hope to honor the deep and profound roots of *indigenous education*. Native American life-ways have always honored the sacred wholeness of children. Traditionally, Indian children came of age with the autonomy to unfold their own gifts, walk their own paths, and choose their own mentors. This way of learning continued into adulthood and Elder-hood as a continuous journey of spiritual growth, a life-long refinement of skills and knowledge, deeply woven with intricate responsibilities to family, clan, the living natural world that sustains the lives of the people, and the spiritual reality sustaining it all.

The story I tell in this book begins after this traditional way of learning has already been intentionally destroyed over centuries by the invading cul-

ture and replaced with a type of education that large-
ly dishonors children. Schools as we know them sep-
arate young people from nature, from family tradition, from spirituality, from mentors, and from one
another. Yet, as I discovered on this journey, a hidden heart of indigenous education lives on. I have
been blessed to witness this heart, and I am called to
share it and do what I can to support its revival.

Today, at the time of this writing, seventeen
years after our paddling journey took place, the spirit
of unity among the indigenous people of this continent (and beyond) makes itself known, in the power
of the historic stand to protect water, land, and sacred
sites from destruction at the hands of the economic,
political, and paramilitary forces of the oil industry.
This story also is not mine to tell. But as a witness, I
see this unity among the Indian Nations like a great
tree standing. Dark waves of greed, violence, and ignorance continue to break upon it, but the tree holds
strong to the earth, extending its roots, opening its
seeds to winds that now arise from all directions.

At this moment in history, this tree stands
most visibly on the great plains, rooted among the
Oceti Sakowin at Standing Rock. The tree stands in
other communities as well, and in the years to come
will root itself in many lands. It stands in harm's
way, and faces violence and ignorance with unity and

prayer, to open a way for all children and future generations ~ that the earth and all its beings may be protected, known, loved, and honored.

The existence of this tree of unity is testimony to its roots: the unimaginable sacrifice and the spiritual endurance of Indian people over the past 500 years. It is also testimony to the spirit of Native youth, whose 2,000-mile run from North Dakota to Washington, D.C. was the catalyst for the current unity of 300 indigenous tribes from across this continent and around the world, standing together to protect the water we all share, as well as Native traditions, human rights, and treaty rights.

In the telling of this story of our small paddling journey into Native North America, may this book I have written be a quiet prayer, an offering of gratitude and support for the life of this tree.

To non-Indian readers of this book:

For European-Americans like myself, to walk a journey of authentic relationship into Indian America requires searing soul-searching. Whether or not we or our direct ancestors perpetrated violence against the original people of this continent is of little consequence. We are heirs to the spoils of our violent history. We burn the dirty fuels of its destructive industries, and we carry its cultural seeds. There is no other path for us than to raise these seeds to full awareness and to relinquish them, through reflection, prayer, and spiritual practice.

The practical choices of our lives, our work, and our relationships matter. We too can stand in support, and turn the cultural tide toward sustainability and compassion. But the choices we make only have power if they are the fruits of our relationship with our deep selves, with our ancestors, with future generations, and with all beings ~ relationships whose essence abides in spirituality. Now is a time to recover the depths and the guidance of the wisdom traditions of our own religions. Because organized religion has so often embodied the ignorance and violence of the dominant culture, we must look deeper, to contemplative and mystical teachings, to the hidden indigenous traditions of our diverse homelands, to practices of mindfulness and compassion, and to the lives of the people of faith who bear these torches. The path of transformation and awakening has many starting points ~ as many, in fact, as there are individual people.

In the face of the violence and tragedy of European-American history, I also seek to give testimony to a quiet parallel story. Because also from the time of the arrival of the earliest European ships, including the ships bearing African slaves, there have been non-indigenous newcomers who have borne a heart for learning and an innate understanding of the unity of the human family. In the face of the immensity of the tragedy, Native people have long welcomed such newcomers into a quiet, heartful, grief-stricken path of transformation through authentic relationship.

Barely discernible in the fabric of our country's history, one can catch the quiet glimmer of the threads of the untold stories of these open-hearted, open-minded newcomers. Many were African-Americans, whose long journeys of suffering intertwined with the lives of Native people, especially in the South. Their stories are passed down through the generations by oral tradition, and their hearts remember.

Yet even among the throngs of white soldiers and missionaries, some of these open-hearted people were soldiers and missionaries. Among the insatiable land-hunger of farmers and ranchers, some of these people were farmers and ranchers. Among the cultural biases of academics and anthropologists, some of these open-minded people were academics and anthropologists. Among the endless ranks of forked-tongued politicians, some of these people were politicians. Among the invading armies of "teachers" of forced acculturation, and social workers enacting the torturous removal of Indian children from their homes and families, some of these people were teachers and social workers.

Over the past 500 years, among the many non-Indians whose hearts and lives have experienced transformation through relationship with Native people, a few chose to stand and speak and act as protectors, to walk this path rather than taking the easy retreat back to the privileges of *Wasicu* society. Some of these men and women laid down their lives on this path. They are not the honored heroes our children learn about in school. But their stories now grow ripe for the telling as we European-Americans claim them and honor them as our own.

As one example: this book is being published on November 29th, the 152nd anniversary of the Sand Creek Massacre in eastern Colorado. Each year, members of the Cheyenne and Arapaho Nations embark on a Spiritual Healing Run/Walk, in remembrance of the 200 people, mostly women and children, who were killed and mutilated by soldiers on the cold morning of November 29, 1864.

But in Denver, the runners stop to honor the graves of two white cavalry officers, Captain Silas Soule and Lieutenant Joseph Cramer, who refused to take part in the massacre, ordering their men not to shoot and allowing people to escape through their lines. Silas Soule, an abolitionist and friend of Walt Whitman, exposed the truth of the massacre by letter and testimony in the weeks that followed, and changed the course of the deceitful war against the plains Indians. He knew he was putting his life at risk. Soon after his marriage at age 26, Silas Soule was shot in the face and killed by another soldier on Larimer Street in Denver. His story fell into obscurity. But the Cheyenne and Arapaho people did not forget him, and today his life is remembered.

So *now*, alongside the life of the great tree of enduring Native tradition and resistance, these glimmering threads of the lives and stories of non-Indians with open hearts and minds are a necessary source of hope. The threads pulse with life, they grow and spread. Our own young people mature in self-awareness, humility, and spirit. They employ the tools at hand, and some stand beside their Native sisters and brothers in the face of violence. They are like an enzyme in the body of the human family, like a yeast of transformation in the non-indigenous world. With our faces to the tree of Native unity and revival, we European-Americans now consider the choice of whether to fully claim our humble tasks, important tasks that only we can accomplish.

~~~

Although I call this story *The Heart of the Canoe,* my students and I did not in fact paddle in dugout canoes, as you will see. But for this book and the educational work that it is spawning, the *Canoe* has metaphorical power. If we consider our complex and rapidly-changing times as a vast river, rising and flowing among rocky islands in swift-moving currents, then we need a pattern for a vessel, for our children and for future generations. Not any vessel can handle such waters.

The vessels we urgently need must be a marriage of old and new forms. The vessels must be alive, with their own spirit and their own heart. Everyone must have a paddle, and a song. Each paddler belongs, in his or her full humanity, with all its vulnerability and power. Each paddler must honor all living beings. Without each person's devotion, grit, humor, creativity, and courageous awareness, the vessel goes nowhere. Yet when we come together, to bring ourselves and one another fully to life, we share in the living heart of the vessel itself, a heart that will guide us, whatever may come.

It is with profound respect that I draw upon the *Canoe* as a pattern and a metaphor for such a vessel. The Native people refer to their paddlers as *Canoe Families,* and such is the quality of their relation-

11

ships. May our schools and our communities have the vision and the courage to undergo the transformation required to embody, in our own unique ways, the heart of the Canoe.

In this story I make a brief reference to *first force, second force,* and *third force.* Without further explanation here, I am referring to a spiritual teaching known as the *Law of Three.* For those interested, there is more about this in my longer forthcoming book, *Living School Design & Practice.*

I have three more deep gratitudes to share. First, teacher and author Eben Heasley inspired me to write this story in the first place, and helped me immensely with skillful and soulful editing support. Thank you, Eben.

Second, Paula *Shell* Nelson is a multi-media artist, singer, songwriter, poet, and Anikituwahgi cultural educator (Eastern Band of Cherokee Indians). I invited her to draw a cover piece for my *Living School* book. To prepare, she read *this* book, and proceeded to create an extraordinary and *uwoduhi* pen-and-ink drawing that is alive with the spirit of the Heart of the Canoe. The piece is too large to fit in this book, but Shell agreed for me to share many small glimpses of this work as the chapter headings. The full work will appear in *Living School Design & Practice. Sgi,* Shell!

And finally: the journey recounted in this story was obsessively all-consuming for me. Even in an ordinary school year, the spouses of teachers shoulder un-sung heavy loads. In 1999, while my students and I were carving paddles and heading out to sea, my wife Rhett was *kicking ass*, working as a nurse in a community clinic in the High Point housing project, caring for our one-year-old son Aidan, and renovating our little West Seattle house. Thank you, Rhett. I am forever grateful.

And thank *you* for reading, for the gift of your attention, whoever and wherever you may be. May you find something useful in these pages. I share this story from a well-rooted conviction that my readers fully possess the courage of heart and spirit to find and forge their path in the larger adventure, together ~ and are already doing so. Such is the blessing of the perilous and beautiful times in which we live.

Chris Weaver
November 29, 2016
Above the North Toe River,
Yancey County, North Carolina

The Heart of the Canoe

Pathfinding

For seven years in the 1990s, I taught at a school called Pathfinder, in West Seattle. Pathfinder was started by a group of parents who applied to the Seattle School District to launch an alternative school with a holistic philosophy and approach. I was a founding teacher, and we enjoyed significant freedom to design our own experiential curriculum. Because of our location, we served a number of urban American Indian and Alaska Native students and families.

Our Native students and parents opened my eyes to a new sense of relationship and a respect for the natural autonomy of children. I remember a student in my first multi-age K-1-2 class, named Celia. She was Tlingit, from the Alaska panhandle. She was a calm and kind-hearted second grader who loved to read to the younger students and to help me with anything I needed. At lunch one November day, Celia told me she would soon be moving to Alaska. I was sad to think she would be leaving. I asked her when, and she said, "I don't know, pretty soon."

The next week I sat down with Celia's mom Ronell for a scheduled parent-teacher conference. I said, "Celia told me that your family's moving to Alaska."

"No, not the family, just Celia. Today was her last day. She's going to live with her uncle on an island near Petersburg. He has a fishing boat."

"How did you decide to send her up there?"

"Celia just wanted to. She's close to her cousins."

"Do you know when she'll be back?"

"No, she will come back down when she wants to come."

I tried to imagine any parents I knew letting a seven-year-old girl decide who in the extended family she wanted to live with, and honoring her choice without a second thought, and I came up blank.

Pathfinder's first principal was a visionary woman named Ramona Curtis. As a girl growing up in that cloudy land of tides and mountains, she had always wanted to be a teacher, but was counseled away from the classroom in college because she spoke with a mild lisp! Undaunted, she became a

beloved and rambunctious P.E. teacher. After suffering injuries in a car accident, she made her way, un-
trained, into a 5th grade classroom teaching position.
Ramona was energetic, brilliant, and strict, with high
standards, a compassionate ear for all her students,
and an unshakable respect for their parents. She was
a big woman with a big voice, imposing as a mother
bear when she needed to be, but full of laughter that
rang down the hallways wherever she worked. She
took her urban kids camping, slogging through estu-
aries, catching critters, singing camp songs around
the fire. She was our visionary leader, a rare and precious blessing.

As she got to know our students, Ramona entered into more and more conversations with the
parents in the Indian community. She heard about
the deep sense of mistrust and alienation that families felt toward the schools, based on the history of
forced acculturation in reservation-based Bureau of
Indian Affairs schools, and the disruptive BIA reloca-
tion programs to cities like Seattle from reservations
all across the west. We had urban Indian students
from the Dakotas and Montana south to Nevada,
along with families from the Coast Salish and other
northwest nations, in addition to Alaska. Most lived
far from their ancestral homelands. Native students
had the highest school dropout rate of any racial

group in Seattle. Scattered widely across the city, Indian families wanted an elementary school that would offer a culture-based curriculum that honored their diverse traditions ~ a school that felt like home.

With the support of our staff and parent community, Ramona entered into a partnership with Dick Basch (Chinook), director of Seattle's Huchoosedah Indian Education Program. They established Pathfinder as a *focus school* for Indian and Alaska Native students. Over the next two years, she recruited and hired Indian teachers, and opened the school to cultural events. Our dear colleague Rita Thomas Bubak (Blackfeet) began a weekly Culture Night, with food, regalia arts, drum-making, singing-and-dancing ~ and, of course, basketball. Each Thursday night the hallways thundered with the sound of Cree Elder Pete Hawley's pow-pow drum, which he led from his wheelchair. Rita also organized bi-annual traditional pow-wows that attracted drum groups from around the Northwest and dancers from dozens of different tribal backgrounds. Our teaching staff developed a culture-based curriculum, understanding that a deep exploration of Native history and traditions would be a rich learning opportunity for Indian and non-Indian students alike.

An Elder storyteller, Ken Jackson (Anishinaabe, whose story-telling name was Grey Eagle), told teaching stories in the cafeteria every Monday morning, playing his hand drum as all the students sat on the green linoleum tile floor. He concluded each session with the kids joining in the refrain: "That's how it *was*, and that's how it *is*." The students returned to their classrooms and interpreted Grey Eagle's stories into writing and art.

Pursuing a culture-based curriculum led to powerful learning experiences for the whole community. One year, an artist-in-residence from the Quinault Nation out on the coast guided our whole school community through our public-school version of a First Salmon Ceremony. Two Native sisters in foster care in our community, Kathy and Krystal, went out with their teachers on a fishing boat in Puget Sound and reeled in the coho salmon for the feast. I was teaching a 2nd-3rd class by then, and we ventured into an urban forest to harvest stinging nettles, wearing latex gloves from our classroom first aid kit, and we cooked nettle soup in two big electric coffee pots in our classroom. The parents came to the feast, and each class had art and songs to share.

The day after, all the students (more than 300) walked a mile in the rain down to Alki Beach to return the bones of the salmon to the waves, to say thank you to the Salmon People. We had learned that, according to Quinault tradition, if there were any twins in the village, having them place the bones in the sea would invite the good fortune of an abundant salmon run the next year, so two kindergarten twin girls in their red raincoats waded out and offered the bones to the little foamy waves, as giant container ships rounded Duwamish Head in the background, heading into port.

With the full diversity of our student body in mind, we held a multi-cultural drum and dance festival one night that featured Indian, West African, Scottish, and Japanese drum and dance groups. There was a powerful moment toward the end when one of the African-American drummers stepped up to the microphone. He told the crowd that his grandmother had passed the oral history of his family down to him as a boy. She told him to always show respect to any Indians he met. Some of his ancestors had escaped from slavery in Georgia, and a Creek Indian village had harbored them for years, placing themselves at risk in the violent years before the Trail of Tears. The Black man addressed the Indian drum groups:

"I have never had an opportunity to publicly say thank you on behalf of my ancestors. I know that you are not from the Creek Nation, but I ask that you receive my gratitude tonight on their behalf." The reply came as a rain of thunder from the big drums.

Ramona invited Elders and Indian community leaders to our school governing site council meetings, to advise us on processes for decision-making (notably Muckleshoot educator Roberta Basch). Pathfinder began using talking circles at all of our site council and staff meetings, to ensure that every voice was heard. Grey Eagle's simple teaching was that taking the extra time results in the right decisions, because "the wisdom comes out of the circle." Interestingly, Pathfinder received its name when an older man literally wandered into one of our talking circles off the street and offered us the name, which he told us was from a legend from Icelandic mythology.

In 1998, the tension in the Seattle School District between centralized and local governance played out at Pathfinder in a challenging way. The school community was deliberating over whether to expand our school from a K-5 elementary school into a K-8 model. With strong opinions on both sides, the community held a talking circle for more than a hundred parents, teachers, and students on a Saturday. The circle took four hours. The resulting decision was to remain a K-5 school. But late in the spring, the district superintendent overturned our community decision and dictated that we expand to K-8, beginning by adding 6th grade the following year. With no additional resources or staffing, I accepted the teaching post for our new 5-6 class of twenty-eight students. Most of our 6th graders were Indian, along with Black, Latino, and Laotian students, as many of the white families opted for more established middle schools.

According to Pathfinder tradition, classrooms chose animals as their "clan names" ~ the first grade *Frog Clan*, the 3-4 *Eagle Clan*, the 5th grade *Bear Clan*. My previous 2-3 had been the *Turtle Clan* for years. In August of the new school year, at the prompting of a wily 6th grader named Gabe Ruiz, my new class voted to become the *Impala Clan*, in honor of the Chevy low-riders with hydraulics that cruised the nearby High Point housing project.

I let it stand. Welcome to middle school.

Cedar Shavings and Dreams

In September, I took the Impalas on a field trip to the Tulalip Indian Reservation north of the city. Our host was a canoe carver named Jerry Jones, and he was at work on a large cedar dugout canoe called *Little Sister*. The kids gathered around the huge form of the canoe emerging from a rare old-growth cedar log. My class was not typically quiet, but in Jerry's presence they dropped into an attentive silence, sitting in piles of cedar shavings on the concrete floor of the shop.

Jerry was a big man. He told us that he had been an aviation mechanic in the Army, and that later as a welder he had built many fishing boats and had helped build the Washington State ferries. But he told us that what we were looking at was not a *boat*.

"A canoe is alive. It is a living being. It is a member of the tribe, and it has a heart. The Elders say that you find the heart in the cedar tree, you uncover it as you are carving, and it lives in the bow, looking forward. When you are at sea, in fog or storms or in the dark, the canoe itself will tell you where to go.

"The traditions of carving these canoes were almost lost. For almost a century the people stopped making them. But in the '80s, the Heiltsuk carvers in Bella Bella revived the art and made a new canoe. From way up in B.C., they paddled to Vancouver. Then David Forlines started carving out at La Push, and the Quileute canoes crossed the open ocean to Neah Bay and Seattle in 1989. At Golden Gardens, Frank Brown challenged all the nations up and down the coast to start carving canoes again and paddle to Bella Bella in four years' time for a ceremony.

"Maybe it sounds romantic. But you need to understand that to carve a canoe takes many months. Paddling to Bella Bella might take a Canoe Family of fifteen pullers eight weeks or more. Many of us have to decide whether to sacrifice our jobs and our income to support our culture.

"Nothing about any of this comes easy.

"In that summer of 1993, twenty-three canoes landed on the beach at Bella Bella for the ceremony. Some of them had paddled more than a thousand miles. And then there were the Makah. All the canoes from the south paddled the inside passage. But the Makah had relatives on the west coast of Vancouver Island, on the open ocean. They are all Nuu-chah-nulth. The US-Canada border split their Nation in two, and it was hard for them to visit each other anymore. The same thing happened to the Haida, with the Alaska border further north. So the Makah decided to paddle the open Pacific on the west coast of Vancouver Island, like in the old days. Some of the biggest waves ever recorded were on that rocky coast. When they landed at the Nuu-chah-nulth village, their relatives picked up the whole canoe, with all the paddlers in it, and carried it to the bighouse.

"A few weeks later, all the twenty-three canoes landed in Bella Bella together. They asked permission to come ashore from the Elders, like in the old days. We had feasts, and ceremony, and shared all our stories. All this happened, just a few years ago."

Jerry paused in his story and looked at one of our Makah students, named Frank. "Some of those paddlers were your age.

"So this canoe, *Little Sister*, is how Tulalip is joining this revival. Tulalip is not like some of the Nations up north, where more of the old ways have carried on. We are a lot of tribes here, on this small reservation: Snohomish, Snoqualmie, Skagit, Suiattle, Samish, Stillaguamish. In the old days each river had its People. So we have to pull it together.

"I wish I could explain to you what it is like to paddle with your People in a living canoe like this. But there is no way to say it in words. To understand it, you have to do it."

Jerry showed us his tools ~ the elbow-adze, the D-adze, the big shipwright's adze ~ just steel blades attached to carved wooden handles. He stood in the canoe and swung the shipwright's adze with his big arms, and the cedar chips flew behind him. He showed us how you remove the wood from the inside until you reach wooden pegs that he put into the hull to gauge the depth. He told us how you steam the canoe with hot rocks and water, which changes the shape; the sides bend outwards, to displace more water and make the canoe stable, and the bow and stern rise up.

The Impalas walked slowly around the canoe, running their hands gently along the gunwales.

~~~

We got back to school in time for "S&R." Our own tradition was to end each rain-free day with Solitude & Reflection ~ the kids would spread out and sit outside on the grassy bank around the basketball court to write in their journals, or just to think. Then we circled up on the blacktop. Many of them had drawn canoes in their journals.

We were quiet for a while until Alyssa, one of the 6th graders, asked, "Do you think *we* could take a paddling trip? Our class? Like he was talking about?"

"I don't know," I said. "We would have to learn a lot. We would need a lot of help. Is that what you want to do?"

Yes. That is what the Impalas wanted to do.

Umiaks

It did not take long for us to realize that we were not going to be able to borrow a dugout canoe. We huddled around a speaker-phone on the floor of the classroom to talk with Peg Ahvakana, the cultural coordinator out at Suquamish.

"Old growth logs are extremely rare, and expensive. But more than that, the whole process of carving a canoe is ceremonially rooted. The canoe is like a member of the tribe, a member of the family. You won't find anyone who would loan one out. But I wonder, have you thought about an umiak?"

She explained that there was another kind of traditional boat revival going on, in a less-sacred context. Its driving force was a guy from New Jersey named Corey. "Go see Corey. He's up in Anacortes."

~~~

Pathfinder School was a few years into being an *Expeditionary Learning School.* As a comprehensive school reform model that began as a part of Outward Bound, EL teachers organize their curriculum into in-depth thematic units called *learning expeditions.* It is the framework of learning expeditions that allowed me to plunge into our dream of a paddling trip. But unlike most learning expeditions, I as the teacher did not know where this one was going.

The opportunities for social studies were obvious. But of course, the standard curriculum content of math, language arts, and science required my time to develop, teach, and assess. As the only 6th grade teacher in the building, I was on my own. That fall was neither the first nor the last time in my career that I have said to myself in exasperation, "This class needs *two* teachers. No, this class needs *three* teachers." So it wasn't until the winter holiday break that I made it up to see Corey.

In 1998, the Skin Boat School was a home-stead-commune of tents and covered sheds, with wood-smoke rising from stovepipes into the rain falling across the wintery green fields. People showed up there, stayed a few months, and built a boat. Corey pulled himself away from showing a woman how to tie off the sinew at the joints of a skeletal wooden frame, and recounted to me a bit of the history of the baidarkas (kayaks) and umiaks.

"Among the traditional Aleuts, the technology and performance of baidarkas was something that we still can't approach, and that no synthetic materials can replicate. Besides wood, they actually integrated the cartilage from sea lions into key joints in the frames, so that in the water, the baidarkas had the flexibility of a sea mammal. For the Aleut paddlers, the baidarka was absolutely an extension of their own body. They spent most of their waking hours at sea.

"Baidarkas have always been built, but the big open boat, the umiak, disappeared. When the Russians colonized the Aleutians in the 1700s, they enslaved the Aleuts to hunt sea otters for them for the fur trade. With an Umiak, people could make war, or a whole village could escape. So the Russian colonizers made possession of an umiak punishable by death."

Corey was walking me over to the back of another building. "So we had to go back to very old historical records to reconstruct the designs. Umiaks are incredibly versatile. They can be all sizes. They can haul an enormous amount of cargo because they ride so high in the water. They can be paddled or sailed, in the passages or in the open ocean. And they are cheap to build. People are just beginning to rediscover the possibilities."

We came around the corner to see an elegant 26-foot craft, upside down, with a beige skin as tight as a drum. "The old ones were covered with sea-lion skins. We use urethane-coated nylon. But the wooden frames are the same." We turned it over to see the benches. The umiak was amazingly light. "There is room for fifteen in this one. You can use it. We can keep it with Meg at the Center for Wooden Boats on Lake Union in Seattle. There's another big one like this that I loaned to a Boy Scout troop down in Olympia, maybe they will let you borrow it. But you need paddles - much longer than canoe paddles. I'll loan you one to use as a template. And you will need to practice on the lake. A lot. Taking an umiak out on salt water is another matter. We will see how your kids do."

Helpers, Songs, and Paddles

Over the next two or three months, I grew to understand the saying that *the universe will rise to meet you*. My wish for two or three teachers was miraculously granted. Ervanna LittleEagle, the mother of a younger Pathfinder student, came on board as a teaching assistant. The Impalas grew to love and trust her quiet patience and warm smile, and her stern look could quell the girl-drama that left me helpless. In March we scored a spirited young VISTA volunteer named Samantha who was a seasoned lake paddler from summer camps in the Boundary Waters of Minnesota. A young Indian man named Ethan also helped out part-time.

More generous support arrived as I started plumbing the depths of the community, asking for help. Vi Hilbert, a renowned linguist from the Skagit Nation, came into the classroom to teach us words in Lushootseed, the language of the Coast Salish Tribes. The remarkable Lower Elwha S'Klallum artist and storyteller Roger Fernandes taught us the fundamental shapes of Coast Salish art and, most precious of all, taught us the *Blackfish Paddle Song*. The song is an honor song to the orca whale, known as *Klumachin* in Lushootseed. Roger played the hand drum, and the Impalas drummed with their hands on the tables and sang. The song's pattern includes three rhythmic deep exhales of air - *Whoooo, Whoooo, Whoooo* - in imitation of the breath from an orca's blow-hole.

I befriended the wood-shop teacher at nearby Madison Middle School, and he got me into the shop one night, which looked like a throwback to the glory days of wood-shops in the 1950s, with its big cast-iron shop tools and a wall full of thirty-year-old hand tools with the blades still sharp. Under cover of darkness I hauled in twenty-eight cedar 2x4s I had bought at Home Depot. Umiak paddle blades are just four inches wide, but I had to settle for three-and-a-half to save money, hoping that they would be able to push enough water. I traced the outline of Corey's paddle on the boards, and spent all night cutting them out on the bandsaw. They emerged as thick, chunky paddle-shapes, with a block handle at one end and a long thick spear-like blade at the other. The wood-shop teacher loaned me a dozen rasps and a dozen block planes to keep in our classroom for a month.

And so, after mornings of writing and doing math, we spent each afternoon carving our paddles. We didn't have clamps, so the students worked in pairs, with one sitting on half of the paddle on the table while the other one worked the plane and the rasp. The floor grew deep in shavings and the smell of cedar filled our whole end of the hall. Little by little, the shafts grew round, the blades grew thin, and the handles took the shape of the kids' hands.

The Impalas divided themselves into two crews, which they named the *Sunrise Crew* and the *Sunset Crew*. They designed a common paddle emblem for each, using the Coast Salish wedges, circles, and crescents Roger had taught us. The kids painted the emblem on one side of each of their paddle blades. The other side they designed individually to represent themselves (initials, skateboards, favorite bands), and they painted those too.

Because I was always helping the kids, I never had time to carve my own paddle. For Ervanna, Samantha, Ethan, and myself, I bought 2x6s to make wider blades, since we would be steering from the stern. One morning I got to school early to get ready for the day. I turned on the lights and looked at my desk, and my eyes opened wide with wonder, and then filled with tears. On top of the piles of paper I saw my own paddle, beautifully carved and sanded, literally glowing. My co-teacher Ervanna had stayed after school into the night to carve it for me.

The Boy Scouts in Olympia agreed to loan us their umiak until summer and I made plans to pick it up over spring break. Corey agreed to haul the other umiak down from Anacortes, and we would meet at the Center for Wooden Boats on Lake Union. The day after spring break, I would bring the Impalas downtown, and we would paddle on the water for the first time.

The students resolved to culminate our study with a four-day paddling trip on Puget Sound, during the last week of school in June. Little by little we developed the route: Depart on Sunday, June 6th, and take the ferry over to Southworth for our launch. Paddle out to Blake Island State Park and spend two nights camped there, practicing all day Monday off the beach to get ready for Tuesday morning, when we would merge with the Bremerton shipping lanes through narrow Rich Passage, clearly the most dangerous part of the route. Camp at Illahee State Park on the Kitsap Peninsula, and paddle our longest day on Wednesday, eleven miles through the strait and across Port Orchard Bay. Our trip would end on the beach at Indianola on the Suquamish Indian reservation. We had gotten to know a carver and basketweaver named Ed Carrier, who had participated in the paddle to Bella Bella in 1993. Ed and his wife Fannie had welcomed us to arrive and stay at their beachfront home. We would spend the last night there and ride the ferry back to Seattle on Thursday. Friday was the last day of school, and that night we would host a celebration for our parents and everyone who had helped.

A parent at Pathfinder owned a 1935 antique yacht named the *Rosalita*, which he rented out for expensive parties on Puget Sound. He volunteered himself and his crew to act as our support boat, and to provide a motorized skiff in case of emergencies. The kids started studying the charts and the tide tables for the days of our trip, to figure out what the currents would be doing.

As all these preparations came together, the magnitude of our endeavor began to sink in. The day before spring break, after S&R, we circled up again on the blacktop. The kids must have known that I had something serious to say, because they were all listening.

"I said something to you guys two months ago, but I realize that I really need to say it again today. When we started this thing, we knew that it might not happen, that it might be impossible. Now we are much further along and we have a lot of helpers and a lot of people pulling for us. But I need you to know that we still don't know if we can do this. We aren't experts. We are way out on a limb. I can think of about ten ways that our plans could end up on the rocks…"

"Don't worry, Mr. Chris," interjected Alyssa, whose idea it was in the first place. She jumped up: "This…is…*happening!*" She spun around. "I can feel it in the wind!"

"It's good to think positive Alyssa. But I need to warn you not to get your heart set on this trip, not a hundred percent. Do you understand what I'm saying?"

The kids nodded, jumped up, and ran back to the building to pack their things for spring break. *Did* they understand? Did *I* understand?

Sunrise and Sunset on the Lake

One day during spring break, with trepidation, I stood outside the downtown office door of the man in charge of insurance and risk management for Seattle Public Schools. I took a few deep breaths, entered, shook his hand, and sat across the desk from him. I told him a little about myself, and I happened to include the fact that my family and I were planning to move to North Carolina that summer. He smiled and said, "I'm a Tar Heel myself." So far, so good.

I explained our plans for the umiak trip: the support boat, the route, our staff, and the story of how the whole thing had come to life. I acknowledged our inexperience with a trip like this, and I gave him an eloquent letter of support from Fannie Carrier at Suquamish, who finished with the words, "When we paddled to Bella Bella in 1993, if we had waited until we knew everything we needed to know before making the journey, our canoe would have never left the beach."

I don't remember the man's name, but I will not forget his smile and his second handshake. "Go forth and do good," he said.

~~~

Pathfinder did not have access to an activity bus, and our parent community, although bravely on board, lacked the time and vehicles to transport us. We would need to ride two articulated city buses to reach Lake Union. So the day after spring break, we walked to the bus stop and stood there, all thirty-two of us, with our sharp six-foot paddle blades pointing to the sky. All the riders' eyes widened as we boarded the bus and took our seats. An inebriated man in the back sat up, blinking and staring, and said, *"Dude, what's with the spears??"*

On the dock, after securing the life vests Meg had handed out, we stepped into the wobbly umiaks. The Impalas were shrieking with excitement and it took a while for us to settle on our benches. From the start, one student in each umiak would sit in the bow facing the crew, and lift the hand drum to play. And we were off, floating (at long last!) across the glassy black water, drifting, clunking our paddles against each other to find a rhythm...and then all at once the umiak would surge forward in one motion, heading across the open water toward the distant bank of Gasworks Park at the north end of the lake.

Ervanna's and my Sunset Crew found its drummer almost immediately. Daniel was a small Shoshone boy from Nevada, and no one else could hold us in rhythm like he could. We were the serious crew, often paddling in silence, and we only sang the traditional songs. Samantha and Ethan's Sunrise Crew sang camp songs, or double-dutch rhymes, or the Brady Bunch theme song, and they were *really* fast. Our Crew consoled itself: "They may be faster, but just wait. We've got *endurance.*"

Twice a week through the rest of April, we made the bus ride to the lake. Most often in the daily spring rains that sift from the low clouds over the Salish Sea, we would paddle for an hour on the smooth gray water to the sound of our drums. At Gasworks Park we would stretch and sit on the wet grass to wolf down our limp, foil-covered lunches from the school cafeteria, and then paddle for another hour before heading back to school.

Each day, we got better.

Return of the Hunt

The spring of 1999 brought with it a dramatic and extraordinary situation, unfolding over many weeks, four hours away at the tip of the Olympic Peninsula in the reservation village of Neah Bay. On the wave of the Canoe revival, the Makah Nation poised itself to revive its ancient tradition of whale hunting by dugout canoe.

For thousands of years, the Makah, who historically occupied a large part of the Olympic Peninsula, hunted the gray whales that migrated by the thousands past Cape Flattery every spring and fall. In the 1855 Treaty of Neah Bay, the Makahs gave up most of their land, but insisted that the treaty guarantee them "The right of taking fish and of whaling or sealing at usual and accustomed grounds and stations." (Treaty of Neah Bay). They became the only tribe in the United States with a treaty expressly guaranteeing the right to whale. However, Makahs did not hunt gray whales after the 1920s, when commercial whaling decimated the population.

By 1994, the population had rebounded and the gray whale was removed from the Endangered Species List. On the wave of the canoe revival, the Makah decided to resume whaling. Supported by the U.S. government, the tribe sought and ultimately won approval from the International Whaling Commission to take up to five gray whales a year.

Makah whaling would be, like many other aspects of the canoe revival, rooted in traditional ways but supported with some modern technologies, as the traditional art of whaling was immensely physically challenging and relied on a life-long development of ancient skills. Traditionally, after a whale was harpooned, sealskin floats were attached, and the whale would tire itself out as it dragged the floats, and the canoe, far out on the open ocean. Once the whale died, it was the task of a particular member of the crew to dive into the waves and, underwater with a large bone needle, literally sew the whale's mouth closed so that its digestive tract would not fill with water and cause the body to sink to the ocean floor.

The paddlers could then tow the whale back to the village, which often was a long journey.

The modern plan included all the ceremonial preparation. The whale would be harpooned from the canoe, hopefully fairly close to shore, and a hunter in a support boat would end the whale's life more quickly with a 50-caliber rifle. As in the old days, the canoe would tow the whale to the beach to be greeted by the village in a ceremonial way.

The Makah decision to resume whaling generated a storm of protest from anti-whaling and animal rights groups. More than 350 groups from 27 countries opposed the hunt. Opponents feared that other indigenous peoples with a whaling tradition would try to follow suit, or that U.S. support for the Makah hunt would weaken efforts to end commercial whaling. One of the most vocal critics was the Sea Shepherd Conservation Society, which threatened to use its fleet to disrupt the hunt. The opponents' initial court challenges were rejected, and the hunt was cleared to begin in the fall of 1998.

Protesters and reporters descended on the Makah reservation, some staying through the whole winter. The whaling crew practiced in their cedar canoe *Hummingbird*, often accompanied by protesters in speedboats. But there was no hunt until spring. Even as the Impalas were practicing on Lake Union, the gray whale migration was underway, and tensions were high at Neah Bay. The unfolding story was all over the headlines of the Seattle Post-Intelligencer.

In the classroom, between our efforts to get ready for the end-of-grade tests, we debated the issue. The Impalas were equally split into treaty-rights and animal-rights camps. I was interested to see that the opinions of my students did not follow racial lines. Even our two Makah students, Frank and Barbie, who had grown up in the city and had never been to their home reservation, were split. In my role as their teacher, I strove to appear impartial myself, and took pride in how the kids thought for themselves.

On the city buses to and from downtown, the kids increasingly entered into conversations with the other riders. Little by little, it was dawning on the Impalas that they were doing something that kids their age didn't usually do. They began to talk to strangers with poise and pride. I remember clearly overhearing a conversation on the bus between Kit, a fifth-grade African-American student on the Sunrise Crew, and a tall, red-haired college student. Kit had thus far been firmly on the animal-rights side. The red-haired man spoke first.

"So, what do you think about the whale hunt?"

"I wouldn't hunt a whale myself," Kit replied. "I think the whales have a right to live. But I wouldn't stop a Makah person from following their tradition."

The young red-haired man replied with irritation: "So, my grandparents are Norwegian, and Norway has a whaling tradition too. Does that mean I can just go out and harpoon a whale?"

"No," replied Kit, calmly.

"Why not?"

"You don't have a treaty."

On the Rocks

As April rolled into May, we got ourselves ready to move from lake training to salt-water training on Elliot Bay. We planned to practice on the bay for the first time on Friday, May 14th. But on Monday, May 10th, the *first force* of our outlandish plans finally encountered an unmovable *second force*. Our umiak journey hit the rocks, in a way that is forever inscribed in my heart.

At the Center for Wooden Boats, Meg was the keeper of our umiaks. She was a strong red-haired woman, a seasoned paddler and a leader of wilderness expeditions. She knew Cory from the Skin-Boat School, and was a colleague of the folks at Northwest Outward Bound. On that afternoon, Meg called me to a meeting in her office.

It happened to be the same day that the Makah whalers took to the ocean and approached a group of gray whales. Their hunt was disrupted by protesters in speedboats, with news helicopters hovering overhead. The *Hummingbird* returned empty-handed.

I had noticed Meg observing us with an increasingly hawk-like eye, and she and I had sparred a bit before. She had expressed her doubts that our young students could paddle an eleven-mile fourth day as planned, if we found ourselves against the wind in the open water north of Bainbridge Island. I had argued that she underestimated the students' determination ("They are not just any-old eleven-and-twelve-year-olds.") She had questioned the depth of our preparations, and I had responded with a confident litany of all our research and the expertise we had on board.

But as soon as I walked in, I knew that today was different. Meg's jaw was set. Her mind was made up.

"The problem is that you don't have in your umiaks the experience to handle what could happen. The weather turns fast, the currents are unpredictable..."

"But the *Rosalita* will be -"

"The *Rosalita* could be well behind you, and there's only one skiff if both boats get in trouble. You don't know salt water, and neither does Samantha or Ervanna. You don't know the currents, and neither of you really knows the umiaks. Rich passage is only 500 yards wide. Container ships and ferries go both ways. What if the wind picks up in the passage, blows you to the edge and you scrape a barnacle-covered rock and rip open the hull? Have you ever stopped a leak in a skin boat in the water?"

I acknowledged that I had not.

"For a trip like this, you need someone *in the umiaks* with real skin-boat experience *at sea*. You don't have it."

Meg sighed and looked at me intently. A wave of deep sadness rose in her eyes, and I was disarmed. For a long moment, she looked at me in silence.

"Chris, I need to tell you a story. Five years ago, a friend of mine was working a sea-kayaking expedition off of Baja, for teenagers. It was a good organization. They were very well prepared and far more experienced than you are. A quick storm came up and their boats got separated in the swells. Four kayaks flipped. Two kids drowned. My friend is the one who pulled their bodies up the beach, and he is the one who had to make those phone calls to those two families. I know he won't ever fully recover, even as the parents and brothers and sisters of the boy and girl who died won't recover. The next time I saw him, I promised myself that part of my job on this earth is to prevent any more of those phone calls from being made.

"You have a lot of passion, you love your kids, you've worked hard. But the sea does not care. You have overestimated your knowledge and your abilities. You are not ready. You can use the umiaks all you want, but they will stay here, on the lake.

"I know you won't be able to hear it, but really, no other students in Seattle even get to do that. I talked to Corey too, and he supports my decision."

I sat in silence, the father of a one-year-old son, tears stinging my eyes, and I knew that she was right.

Third Force Wears a Leather Jacket

I slept fitfully that night, imagining telling the kids, staring in the face of this massive betrayal, my months of obsession without my feet really on the ground, the arrogance of appointing myself as the captain of an umiak full of children, the fragile shoots of hope that I had coaxed out into the air, only to be frozen in utter disappointment, as happens again and again in the lives of children growing up in places like High Point, or children growing up anywhere else for that matter.

In the classroom in the morning, as the Impalas prepared to paddle one last day on Lake Union, I started to tell them the news, but I couldn't. The words caught in my throat. I watched our rag-tag class of urban pre-teens moving with a unified energy around the classroom and halls, gathering their paddles and gear and bus money, joking and laughing. They hardly noticed me as we boarded the bus and rode through the city on a morning of sun through bleak high clouds.

Watching me on the bus, Ervanna guessed, and asked me with her eyes; all I could say was, "I'll tell you later." We piled into the umiaks, and I was grateful to be at the back of the boat with Daniel in the bow, pulling through the dark lake-water, one drumbeat at a time.

~~~

Ninety minutes later, I got us off the lake early. We had fifteen minutes before the bus would arrive, and I figured it was enough time for me to tell them the news; I didn't want *too* much time. Somehow, paddling to Daniel's drum, the sound of the water, the words of the song had carried me to a place of acceptance. I had prepared what to say in my mind, how to take responsibility for the decision myself. I would not blame Meg, and I would not tell Meg's story, which was not my story to tell.

The Impalas were running around on the grass. As I drew breath to call them in, a girl's voice cried out in pain. Asia, a tall, athletic dancer on the Sunrise Crew, had sprained her ankle, badly. She leaned on Kari and Krystal and limped over to the bench of a wooden gazebo, where she sat crying as Kari took off her shoe. Asia's ankle was already starting to swell. Samantha wrapped it carefully and went across the street to get some ice. The bus we were going to catch pulled away from the stop and moved on. The Impalas sat around on the grass. Blond-haired Eli, our skateboarder, picked up the hand drum and started playing softly, singing our paddling song.

The air was still as ether.

A man walked our way from Fairview Avenue. He came on over and stood at ease near Eli, Asia, and Kari on the bench. We did not know him. He was Indian, a little rough-looking, wearing a black leather jacket and a bone-bead choker. He looked around at the kids, the pile of paddles on the grass, Asia sitting on the bench.

"What song is that?"

"Blackfish Paddle Song," replied Eli, softly drumming still. "Jamestown S'Klallam."

The man nodded. "What are you guys doing here?"

When I answered him, I spoke softly and deliberately, but I heard my own words as if from another place, as if my brain was no longer connected to my own mouth:

"This is the Impala Clan, from Pathfinder School in West Seattle. In three weeks, they are going to paddle for four days, from Southworth to Suquamish."

Again, a nod. I heard myself continue, and this time I was genuinely surprised at the words coming out of my mouth:

"Tell me: Are you doing anything from the sixth to the tenth of June?"

The man looked at me. "I don't believe I have any plans."

"Tell us," I went on. "Do you know anything about skin-covered boats?"

One corner of his mouth went up, along with his eyebrows, and he gave me an extended glance. "Yes, I know about skin-covered boats. My father used to build umiaks, and I built one myself. Ten years ago I was a student for a while at a school called Warren Wilson College in North Carolina. For spring break my buddy and I sailed my umiak from Wilmington through the Outer Banks, all the way up Chesapeake Bay."

~~~

And so it happened, exactly like that. His name was Peter Skerrat. In the next five minutes, I explained to him our full circumstance (I remember seeing Sean and red-haired Kari exchange shocked looks when they heard that our umiaks were currently hostage on the lake). I asked Peter if he would captain the Sunset Crew, including on our salt-water training days, and he agreed. I asked if he would walk over to the Center for Wooden Boats and talk to Meg, and he said "Sure," and shook my hand.

We carried Asia across the grass and caught the next bus back to school, where the students had to dash and scramble to get to their yellow buses in time. By the time I got home, Meg's voice was on the answering machine, friendly and a little bit dazed, letting me know that we had the green light.

"I don't know how you found him, but he's an expert, more-so than me. Honestly Chris, how many people have built an umiak and taken it to sea? I'm surprised that Peter even exists. But I'm happy for you guys."

And at 5am on Friday morning, very much in existence, Peter met me with his truck at Lake Union. We each towed an umiak on its trailer across the West Seattle Bridge to Seacrest Park, where later that morning we would begin our salt-water training on the windy, rainy waters of Elliott Bay.

Potlatch

Early on the morning of Monday, May 17th, before any protest boats appeared, the Makah whalers harpooned and killed a 30-foot gray whale, for the first time in seventy years. The harpooned whale pulled the canoe for several minutes until it was killed by a rifle shot from a Makah hunter on the support boat. The *Hummingbird* towed the whale to shore, accompanied by canoes from visiting tribes. The whale was carved on the beach in the rain amid a large gathering of people, and Makahs of all ages ate fresh blubber, all but the oldest for the first time.

Ervanna LittleEagle made the four-hour drive to Neah Bay for the Makah Potlatch ceremony over the next weekend. There were guests from all up and down the coast, as well as indigenous people from all over the world, including a Masai contingent from Kenya and a group from Fiji. When she returned, she told us many stories, with the Impalas gathered on the floor in rapt attention.

Ervanna told us about a story shared by Billy Frank Jr, a Nisqually environmental and treaty rights leader. In describing the relationship between the Makahs and the whales, he told how a gray whale would sometimes come to the beach and lie on the sand, half in the water, as if bearing a message, and then it would slide itself back into the sea. He described how, whenever a whale would get caught in Makah fishing nets, the fishermen would dive in and unwrap the whale from the net so it could go on its way.

Ervanna told us how the captain of the U.S. Coast Guard boat was at the Potlatch, and that the room reverberated with applause when Billy Frank Jr. thanked the Coast Guard for upholding the Makah's treaty rights. Ervanna shared how she spoke with one of the hunters from the *Hummingbird*, and that he told her the story that the night before the hunt, in ceremony, the whale itself had told an Elder when and where it would rise in the morning.

But the most entrancing story was from the words of a Fijian woman who spoke at the microphone to the whole gathering. She honored the Makah hunters for persevering to bring about a "spiritual event in the life of the world," and then she told the story of the whaling tradition on her south Pacific island home.

Traditionally, Fijian women were considered to be the whalers, and this role was passed down from generation to generation. The storyteller herself wore the ceremonial dress of this lineage. She told that in the old days, the women learned whale songs, and when the people were in need, the whale women would walk out to a point, high above the ocean. They would sing the whale song, and sing, and sing, and the rest of the people would stand behind them in silence. After a while, the whales would come. They would gather at the point, and breach and listen. Eventually, one whale would make a decision to give itself to the people for their sustenance. This whale would *beach itself*, with the other whales close behind, out in the water. The whale women would walk the trail down to the beach, singing all the while, and would gather around the whale, and put their hands on it, and sit on the sand around it and sing, until, as the woman told, the whale's spirit would rise to the sky. Then the whale meat would be shared among all the people.

Alyssa and the Whale

Alyssa was in sixth grade for her Impala year, on the Sunrise Crew. She is the one who first asked me if we could take a paddling trip, and I am quite sure that without her presence, our journey would never have happened. It is interesting that we ended up paddling umiaks, which among us all were only Alyssa's inheritance, through her Aleut grandmother, Barbara. As much as any real story can have a beginning and an end (which, in truth, it can't), Alyssa stands at both, our *Alpha* and *Omega*.

She is the most impulsive child I have ever taught. One Saturday, when she was in third or fourth grade, I picked her up with her younger cousin Mykki in the Huchoosedah van. Alyssa was riding shotgun. We were going to a drum-making workshop at Pathfinder, and the next student I was picking up was Daniel (not our umiak drummer but a different one). I got to Daniel's house, left the girls in the van, and walked up to the porch. As I was talking to Daniel's mom, Alyssa reached across and popped the van out of park into neutral. The van was on a hill and started rolling backwards. Alyssa screamed and climbed like a spider-monkey out the passenger-side window and leaped out onto the grass. I chased the van, with Mykki still in the back seat, twenty feet down the hill and was able to jump in and hit the brakes. That is Alyssa.

She lived with her grandma Barbara. Alyssa once told me that she was Indian, Black, Japanese, and Irish. The world's child. In sixth grade she was always talking, laughing, singing, dancing. She would get fiercely up in the face of the most aggressive boys. She compulsively stole things and had to be on a behavior contract that mandated a suspension if she was caught with anything belonging to anybody else. Volatile, yes, but as many other middle school teachers will understand, Alyssa was also our energy source, our raw flame, our live wire, our rocket fuel. She was intuitive and would call out answers before anyone else had gotten their head around the question. One day she would power through her math work, and the next day she wouldn't have anything to do with it because her mind was somewhere else. Alyssa could fill a teacher's heart with hope, and dash it on the rocks a moment later. Without meaning to I developed a facial expression just for her. My Alyssa-face: disbelief, exasperation, scolding and love, in equal measure.

~~~

Already in the second week of saltwater training, I was thinking about what Cory had said about it being another world entirely. The afternoon was cool and drizzly, and just launching from the beach without a dock was a challenge, as the kids stood knee-deep in the water to climb over the rails while their crew-mates held the umiak steady. The paddlers were shivering by the time we were all afloat. The wind buffeted us in circles, and flocks of waves from the wakes of the ships on the bay bounced us around.

With Peter at the stern, I got to pull from the side, and we paddlers sang louder, and dug deeper, and after a while we were traveling north along the beach. The sight of the Sunrise Crew struggling nearby was no longer a call to competition but instead a great comfort, as the wind rose and the green-gray water heaved and rolled with an entirely different life from the lake we knew.

The wind picked up. It was slow going, the kids seemed to be slacking off, and Peter and Samantha were both frustrated. When we got back to the beach, we pulled the umiaks up and decided to circle up on the grass above the wall to debrief. It was mid-afternoon, and we had about forty-five minutes before we needed to catch the city bus.

In the middle of our debrief, a woman standing at the rail on the wall shouted, *"A whale, it's a whale!"* We all got up and ran to the wall, expecting to see the tall black fin of an orca, a rare enough sight in Elliott Bay. But perhaps fifty yards out, the long back of a much larger whale rose from the water, followed by the enormous flukes of its tail. The Impalas dropped over the wall to the beach. The gray whale was moving north toward Duwamish head, traveling fast. The kids ran up the beach until they hit the end of Seacrest Park. The whale kept going, and so did we, dodging under the barnacled pylons of the West Scattle ferry dock and clambering over boulders and break-walls toward Duwamish Head. Near the point, there was a small sand beach, and we congregated there, out of breath, scanning the empty water.

Alyssa strode out into the water until she was knee-deep, and started singing the Blackfish Paddle Song in a clear, mighty voice. Two more students followed. We all lost our breath when the whale breached directly in front of us, not far from shore. The Impalas started singing again, and a moment later it breached again, closer still, launching half of its magnificent body into the sky and hitting the water in an explosion of foam. The whale stayed, breaching and breaching, closer and closer, until it was impossible to believe that the water could be deep enough. We could see the white patches on the whale's jaw, the sleek brown-gray skin beneath, and its small eye, turned toward the beach. Ten strong swimming strokes and I could have put my hands on its skin.

For at least twenty minutes, we stayed just like that, many of the Impalas standing waist-deep in the water, abiding in the sound of our song and the rhythmic sight of the breaching whale. Finally, one of the kids asked me, "Don't we have to catch the bus?" and we stepped out of the dream. Samantha took half the kids and ran back to Seacrest to get our packs. Peter said he would put all the paddles in his truck. When Samantha got back, we had four or five minutes before the bus would arrive.

Seven kids were still standing in the water singing, and the whale was still breaching. I called them to come back to the sand, but they didn't even turn, except Alyssa, who ran through the water and stood facing me.

"We can't go!"

"But we have to go, you'll miss the bus home. We've watched a long time!"

"Don't you see? We can't go! If she beaches herself we need to be here, *she needs us to be here to sit around her and sing while she's dying!*"

In that moment, the vision of Alyssa filled my whole being: fierce as a tigress, her purple T-shirt wet with seawater halfway up, her black hair whipping in the wind, black eyes blazing, standing her ground in the sand.

She misinterpreted my silence. "WE'RE NOT GOING!" she shouted.

"I'll stay with them," called Samantha from behind me.

"Okay!" I said. "I'll call their parents from school and I'll pick you guys up. But it's going to be a while!" Alyssa was already back in the water, and I took note of who her six companions were (all girls, except Daniel our drummer from Nevada), and herded the rest of the Impalas up to the road.

It is an indulgence of the storyteller, but today I think: if instead of getting on the bus I had been run over by it, and had found myself with a crushed ribcage, lying on the pavement looking up at the sky, I would have drawn my last breath in contentment, I would have thought my final thought like a spoonful of honey:

This is enough, I can go, I am ready to go,
because I have seen the World's Child,
I have beheld her with my own two eyes.

On the bus ride back to school I was sitting across the aisle from Tina, a slight fifth grader whose dad was from Laos.

"Hey Mr. Chris."

"Yeah?"

"That whale. She's not going to beach herself."

"Oh? How do you know?"

"She can't. The tide's coming in. High tide's not till six."

~~~

Back at school, after the Impalas boarded their buses, I gave the names of the seven whale-singers to Carrie at the front desk. "Just call home, tell their parents that they are at the beach watching a whale, and that I'll bring them home. Pretty soon. For sure

66

before six." I swapped my truck for a teacher-friend's minivan and headed back down to Duwamish Head.

Tina was right, of course. The whale had stayed for another fifteen minutes, and then had turned and headed out toward the middle of the Salish Sea, bearing northwest. Samantha was on the beach, throwing a frisbee with the whale-singers, except Alyssa, who chattered at me while she was using a long skinny piece of driftwood to try and retrieve her cell phone, which she had dropped behind a jumble of boulders against the concrete wall.

"I hope she didn't mind that we were singing the *orca* song. She was probably offended. They probably don't get along."

"How do you know it was a *she*?"

"Shut up, of course she's a she. And you should have seen, when she finally left, she blew a bunch of water out her blowhole. That is *goodbye* in her language. Just her language for *people* though, she can just sing whale words to her whale friends, underwater."

The Heart of the Canoe

If this story is a Canoe, then the Canoe has a heart, and the heart of this story-Canoe knows where it is going.

I am not the only one paddling but I reckon I have a steering paddle, and at this midway point of the journey, I must steer us to a small beach before moving on. I have to step out, if only for a moment. Shake out my hands, walk a bit.

Carver Jerry Jones said, "Nothing about any of this comes easy," and he is telling the truth. The heart of this story-Canoe knows where it is going, but my own heart does not want to go there, my own heart is digging in its heels in the salty-wet sand until I can no longer see the words I am writing.

But all of us who have journeyed with children and seen them grow, and grown with them, and then let them go to make their way into the unpredictable world know that this is how it is sometimes. This is part of the deal.

The Canoe knows where it is going. We breathe, we reach deep and trust, and we get back in. We put our paddles in the water.

Or if we can't even do that, we surrender ourselves to the inexorable pull of the current on the heart of the Canoe.

Red Cloth in the Fire

The Impalas' parents gave us a send-off at the Fauntleroy ferry dock, with hugs and well-wishes and a trust that filled my heart. Peter and I towed the umiaks onto the car deck, and the kids raided the snack bar and then stood at the rails on the upper deck in the wind, looking out at the islands.

We set out from the gravel beach at South-worth, paddling strong across the choppy waves toward Blake Island with the diesel-powered *Rosalita* close behind. By now the Impalas were accustomed to their positions. They watched the backs of the kids in front of them, following the sound of the drum, plunging their painted cedar paddles into green water that was far darker and deeper than we had ever ridden before.

We made the crossing in good time. When

our Sunset Crew umiak felt the gravel of the beach on the hull we lifted our paddles to the sky. The Sunrise Crew was already on the beach, and Eli shouted, *"Dudes, what's with the spears??"*

We carried the umiaks up above the driftwood line and flipped them over for the night. After making camp and cooking hot dogs, the Impalas settled into their tents, scattered along the edge of the woods. The waves lapped on the rocks as the flashlights in the tents went out, one by one.

The next day after breakfast we trained in the waves over three sessions, picking landmarks on the coastline of the island and racing to reach them. The crews had a rotation so that everyone had a chance to get aboard the *Rosalita* and ride on the skiff, but a few of the students ~ Frank, Barbie, Sean ~ passed up their turns, because they had made personal pacts to paddle the whole journey without a break. The Impalas laughed and argued and splashed their way through the day, but all the while we were aware of the narrow entrance to Rich Passage across the water, which we would enter the next morning.

That night, Peter found a place deeper in the woods to have a simple ceremonial fire. He told a couple of stories and then laid down the talking stick and opened it up for the kids to say anything that was on their hearts. Our sixth graders, many of whom lived in the High Point housing project, began sharing stories about the hard situations that lay ahead for them in the summer, once school was out. They talked about things they had never told each other about their lives - older brothers in gangs, fathers in prison, family members with HIV. I remember our fifth graders, more of whom were white and lived in middle-class neighborhoods, listening to the kids from High Point as if they were telling tales from another world, although that other world was just ten or twenty blocks away from their doorsteps.

The silences grew longer. A white boy named Sean picked up the stick. He started talking but it was hard for him to get the words out. He said, "There are just some things I said recently. I just wish I could go back and change it. I wish I could go back and edit things, you know?" There were tears on his cheeks in the firelight.

Peter produced a red strip of cloth and placed it in the fire. It flared and lit up the branches of the pine trees above our heads. "Sean, you understand the power of your words. And you are right to think that every word you say matters, every word counts. But you can trust that what you feel now is the Creator working through your heart. There is nothing that we say or do that can't be reconciled. We just have to ask for forgiveness and to be shown the right path. We have to be humble and keep listening. And then we have to use our own will to do what we are guided to do."

Ashes in my Mouth

We were up early to break camp and catch the incoming tide into the passage. As the Umiaks drew near the southern edge of Bainbridge Island, the Bremerton Ferry from Seattle came into sight, still far in the distance. The biggest of the fleet, the ship was enormous, carrying hundreds of cars below its passenger decks. Samantha and Peter signaled one another that they could make it across the lanes, and the paddlers dug in. But a minute later the *Rosalita* blew its horn, thinking the ferry was closing too fast. We back-paddled, and then held our position. The ferry sounded its horn and we knew the captain had seen us. The big ship passed very close, between us and the island, and the Impalas started waving their paddles up at the passengers on the deck.

Then all at once the waves from the wake were on us. Peter steered us into the first wave, which we rode, but we dropped into the trough and the second wave broke over the bow into our laps. The crew shouted and kept paddling, and we saw the other Umiak turn on the first wave and take the second one over the starboard side before turning bow-first into the next wave. The Impalas were breathless and whooping with excitement as we rode the rest of the waves and slipped into the current, strong as a river, heading into the narrows. We bailed out the water with buckets as the rocks and trees on the shore slid past.

Only two ships passed us in the passage, and Samantha and Peter held us expertly to the side, but not too close to the rocks. When we came out of the passage an hour later and could ease our concentration, the tide turned and we had to paddle harder into the afternoon to reach our campsite. We got to the state park by 3:00. Most of the kids took a hike with the teachers, but a few of them stayed to hang out on the *Rosalita*, which was tied to the dock.

When we got back from the hike, one of the men from the *Rosalita* pulled me aside to tell me something. I listened in disbelief. He said he had caught Alyssa trying to start a fire on the yacht's deck with a lighter.

"Starting a *fire*?"

"Yeah, she had even grabbed a handful of sticks from the shore."

I was fuming. I found her and marched her down the beach.

"Alyssa, are you out of your mind?? What were you thinking??"

She kicked at the rocks. "I don't know! And you wouldn't understand anyhow."

"There's *nothing* to understand! Those guys are giving a week of their time to us, away from their own kids! We couldn't even be taking this trip if not for them! Not to mention that boat must be worth a half a million dollars!"

She shot me a smoldering look and started throwing rocks into the water. After a while she said, "I heard them talking about us."

I grabbed her by the shoulders and turned her to face me.

"Dammit Alyssa, grow up! I need you to walk up there and apologize. And tomorrow morning, you are grounded. You can ride with the ground crew. You can meet the umiaks at lunch."

She was undaunted. "Who's going to be with me?"

"I am! Otherwise who knows what you'll decide to do."

She threw rocks for five more minutes while I waited, and then she turned to face me. She pointed across the water at the expensive homes above the beach on Bainbridge Island.

"All those fancy houses. All these ships. Do they own the water? Who owns this water, anyway?"

Alyssa turned and walked up the beach, across the dock, and onto the yacht to talk to its crew.

~~~

The next morning, the world looked numbingly wrong from the window of the car: the signs, the gravel lots, the logging trucks. Finally we pulled up to the beach where we were going to meet for lunch. Alyssa helped me unpack the food and make peanut butter sandwiches, but we didn't talk much. We sat on the wall for an hour, waiting for the paddlers to come into view. Neither one of us could think of anything to say. I felt like I had ashes in my mouth.

At last the sound of the hand drums reached us, followed by the sight of Alyssa's classmates, moving toward us across the gray water. The Impalas pulled up on the beach, noisy and ready for their sandwiches, and carried the umiaks up onto the gravel. I ate by myself, while Samantha took Alyssa for a long walk down the beach.

A Song across the Water

After lunch we launched the umiaks from the gravel beach for the longest stretch of this longest last day on the water. With the Kitsap Peninsula on our left and Bainbridge Island on our right, we would paddle the rest of the strait and then cross the large open expanse of Port Orchard Bay to the Carriers' beach in Indianola. The sunlight was flat, the water calm with small wind-driven riffles. Alyssa was back with Samantha and the Sunrise crew, pulling hard.

The day wore on, stroke by stroke, and little by little the clouds moved over us. In the distance I could see sunlight glinting off the waves beyond the edge of the clouds. Daniel was drumming, but no one was singing. I fell into a bit of a trance, and for a moment I thought I heard a song, coming across the water. I sat up and listened harder.

All at once Peter said, "Daniel, stop drumming. Paddlers, rest!" We drifted in silence.

"See, we've got *endurance*," Krystal said, pointing at the Sunrise Crew which was forty yards back.

"Shhhhhh!" said Peter, "*Listen.*"

It *was* a song. A woman's voice, and a drum, a language we didn't know, traveling across the water like a hummingbird in flight.

"Forward!" called Peter. We paddled in silence, listening and looking, following the sound of the song. After many minutes, Daniel said "There!" and pointed. I could see three small figures on a gravel beach on the left-hand side of the strait. It seemed impossible that the sound could travel so far, but now the song and the drum had grown clear.

"They're drumming us in," said Peter.

The three women stood, in traditional dress and woven cedar-bark hats. The one in the middle had graying hair shining in the sun as she struck the hand drum.

~~~

In the classroom, a month before, we read an account of the arrival ceremony that had been revived for the paddle to Bella Bella. Traditionally, any canoe that approached a village needed to gain permission to land, to announce that they were not foe but friend. An Elder would call from the beach, and ask who it was who approached their home. A representative from the canoe would stand, and there were protocols of what to say, and how.

The account we read was from Al Charles Jr, the skipper of the Elwha S'Klallam canoe from Port Angeles. His canoe had a remarkable story. When the time arrived for the paddle to Bella Bella, their canoe was not finished. The final step was to attach two large pieces of cedar to form the raised prow and stern. But they embarked anyway, and their eight pullers crossed into Canada and made their way north. At each village they visited on the route, the carvers there offered to help, and over the course of the journey, the Elwha S'Klallam canoe was completed by the hands of people in the other villages, tribes who had once been their enemies.

At Bella Bella, the Heiltsuk Elders called out to the canoes, to ask them who they were. Al Charles Jr. called in reply with these words, as he stood in the stern of the canoe off the beach:

We are the Elwha S'Klallam Nation. In the name of the Creator of all good things, we come in peace. We have traveled a great distance to be with you, to honor your people, to respect your waters and to know this land. We bring greetings from our nations to the south. Like our ancestors, we move carefully on this voyage. We have learned some things and we have come to share with your people so we can learn more. Our hearts are filled with love for you. May we have permission to come ashore?

Although we had drawn inspiration from the stories, we knew that we were not a *Canoe Family*, and the Impalas were not a *People*. We had never imagined that we would be drummed-in and welcomed by anyone. Yet before us on the beach stood Suquamish Elders, who somehow had known that we were coming. How did they know?

And we hadn't practiced our part.

As the umiaks drew closer to shore, Peter said, "They're going to ask us who we are." He looked at our twelve-year-old Makah paddler, Frank. "Frank, will you speak for us?" He nodded.

A moment later, the woman's voice called across the water. The song had ended and her voice was stern, it rang like a challenge:

"Who are you? What brings you to the shores of the Suquamish Nation?"

In one motion everyone in the Sunrise crew's umiak looked over at us. In his place toward the

81

stern, Frank stood up tall and faced the women on the beach.

"*I am Frank Mather. I am Makah. We are the Impala Clan from Pathfinder School. We are the Sunset Crew, and this,*" gesturing to our sister umiak, "*is the Sunrise Crew. We come in peace. We come with respect and with gratitude. May we have permission to come ashore?*"

The woman in the middle answered with a flurry of drum beats, and called out, "You are welcome here in our land! You may come ashore."

~~~

The drummer was Peg Ahvakana, the Suquamish Cultural Coordinator, who had advised us by speaker-phone back in October to look into borrowing an umiak. Fannie Carrier had told her of our planned itinerary, and she had chosen this beach below the Suquamish Cultural Center for their welcome, but she had kept it as a surprise. We will not forget the gift. Her generosity of heart and power of voice had invited us into an unforgettable moment out of time.

Yet the half-hour or so that we spent on her beach was awkward. The Impalas were horsing around on the beach. Peg and her companions invited us into the Cultural Center museum, and the kids walked through, chattering and laughing loudly and not paying much attention to the displays. As we stood in the museum lobby, Ervanna leaned over to me and said, "Being in the umiaks is one thing. But when they step ashore, our kids don't really know how to act."

We thanked Peg and her companions as we prepared to board the umiaks again, but I was thinking about Ervanna's words. The umiaks gave us a container, they held us together. But outside the umiaks, what kind of container did we have? Without our paddles in our hands, what did we have to hold us together?

The Return

Our final two hours of paddling were bitter-sweet and glorious. The late afternoon sun angled through broken clouds as the Sunrise crew and the Sunset crew headed out into the open waters of Port Orchard Bay. We had the foil of a steady headwind from the north, which forced the Impalas to do their best work, because without all our muscles pulling in unison, there was no headway to be made. Whenever we stopped to rest we drifted backwards. But the two umiaks found their zone, and we stayed side-by-side, with even the two hand-drums beating as one. The sun caught the drops of water spraying off the ends of the kids' paddles as they arose from the sea in one motion to swing forward in an arc and re-enter the water. We sang in the wind until our voices were hoarse.

The shore ahead drew closer little by little, until at last we were close enough to see all the landmarks. We paralleled the beach, looking for the house and yard that Fannie had described to me. Finally, we saw Ed and Fannie walking down the wooden steps and out across the rocks, waving to greet us.

Our evening at the Carriers was quiet and sweet. While Ed was grilling burgers for us, the weary Impalas rested on the grass of the yard or flipped rocks in the tide-pools looking for crabs. The teachers sat with Ed and Fannie and told them the story of the journey. We decided not to set up our tents but instead to sleep on the grass under the stars, and the Carriers let some of the kids sleep on their living-room floor. We slept deeply under the sky, where the winds flowed freely over sea and land toward their horizons that never end.

~~~

Morning brought the harsh reality of our immense transition as we began to pack our things. We realized that in many ways we had not thought or planned beyond this moment in time. The ground crew was bringing the Huchoosedah vans to drive us to the ferry and back to school. I realized that I didn't even have money for the ferry tickets, and

Fannie had to give us $50 so we could get the Impalas across the sound and back to Pathfinder. Tomorrow was the last day of school. We had invited all our parents and everyone who had helped us to a celebration in the cafeteria, but we had not had time to plan any of it.

Ethan drove my truck with the Sunset umiak so I could ride in the van. We were so tired that a lot of the Impalas and I slept away the van ride, with many of them still dreaming in their seats on the car deck during the ferry crossing.

We entered the front doors at Pathfinder at 2pm, less triumphant than exhausted. School as usual ~ the younger students in class at their tables or moving about the halls, kindergarteners on the playground, a teacher carrying a pile of notebooks ~ seemed so strange as to be almost unrecognizable. When people asked us in the hallways, "How was your trip?" we heard ourselves saying, "It was great," or simply, "Fine."

The classroom was strange too, with books and papers and lunch boxes strewn around. The Impalas were cranky but I gave them no direction. I stood looking at my desk. It was heaped with piles of un-graded papers. The bottom desk drawer was standing open to reveal a loose thick stack of dollar bills, $140 that I had collected from the families for a field trip a month earlier that we had needed to cancel. *"At least I can pay Fannie back for the ferry tickets,"* I thought.

The minutes slipped by and the kids were gathering their things. Some of them were eager to see their parents who were soon to pick them up, but many others were getting ready to board their yellow buses, as if it was just another school day. Under it all, like a steady ache, was the rising realization that after tomorrow, we would not see each other again for a long time, maybe ever. The thought felt like an unexpected sentence from an unseen judge for a crime we hadn't committed.

I moved some books from my chair, dropped them on the floor, and sat behind my desk. Ervanna came by and asked, "Chris, have you made any plans for the food for tomorrow night?" I put my hands on my head and grabbed my hair, which she expected, and she smiled at me and said, "We'll figure it out."

As half of the kids were bringing their things to their tables to wait for the announcement of the end of the school day on the PA system, Gabe walked up to me. "Mr. Chris," he said, "Alyssa just stole my CD from my locker. Willie saw her put it in her backpack."

I sighed. "Okay Gabe, I'll deal with it."

I sat there numbly and followed painful thoughts. Alyssa's behavior contract meant she should be suspended from school tomorrow. I tasted again the ashes in my mouth, and like a stab in the gut I realized that if she was suspended tomorrow, Alyssa probably wouldn't even come to the celebration in the evening. I felt like the Impalas' whole year together was unraveling and slipping through my fingers like water, onto the floor and down the drain.

I closed my eyes and took a deep breath, and something flared in the back of my mind, a red strip of cloth, lighting up the pine boughs that were suddenly overhead against a sky full of stars. I opened my eyes and jumped up from my chair. I walked to the door, where Alyssa and Willie were arguing in the hallway.

"Alyssa, come in here to my desk," I said.

A moment later she was standing next to me, looking at the ground.

"Alyssa. You stole Gabe's CD."

"Yes."

"You need to give it back."

"I already did." She was still looking down.

"You know that you need to be suspended tomorrow."

A pause. "Yes."

"Alyssa, look at me." She looked up. Her eyes were unreadably distant, but I held my eyes on hers. "If I give you $140 in cash right now, will you come to school tomorrow evening at 5 o'clock, and be ready to feed a hundred people at six?"

All at once she was back, her eyes on mine widening for a moment, then looking up at the ceiling, then back down to meet my look.

"Yes."

Carrie's voice on the PA announced end of the day. I reached down, dug out the cash, and placed it in Alyssa's hand. She spun out the door and ran down the hall toward the bus lines.

Klumachin's Breath

The next morning, before the Impalas got to work planning our celebration, I stood and faced them at their tables.

"Impalas, I have a question for you.

"Yesterday afternoon, I told Alyssa that she was suspended today for stealing Gabe's CD. I also gave her $140 in cash, and I asked her to arrive at school this evening at five, to be ready to feed all of our guests at six. She said that she would."

Some of the students exchanged looks. I went on.

"My question for you is, *do we need a backup plan?* We could order enough pizza for everyone and pay for it somehow. I want to know what you think."

I expected an eruption of talk, but nobody said anything for fifteen seconds. Then, it was Gabe:

"We don't need a backup plan."

Everybody nodded, and we started our last day of school.

~~~

A few minutes before 5:00 that evening, Frank and Barbie, who had stayed after school, and Ervanna and I were finishing setting up the chairs in the cafeteria. A few other Impalas who had volunteered to arrive by five to help started trickling in.

Alyssa's grandma Barbara's van pulled up in front of the school. Alyssa slid the side door open, and started carrying things in. She had four deep aluminum trays full of white rice and gumbo, and some big bowls with giant balls of dough for fry-bread. Alyssa took charge of the kitchen, putting the gumbo in the ovens to stay warm and filling three electric skillets with oil. She and Frank and Barbie cooked the fry-bread and stacked it into towers on the counter, with paper towels in between each one. The other kids mixed big drink coolers with powdered lemonade. Any time Ervanna or I approached the doors, Alyssa would shout "Nope! Stay out of the kitchen!"

The guests started to arrive, and right at 6:00, Elder Vi Hilbert said a prayer in Lushootseed. The

Impalas followed according to the tradition that Rita had taught us at Culture Night, by bringing plates out to give to all the Elders first. Then all the parents, teachers, students, and guests went through the serving line, where Alyssa chattered away at everyone, spooning out the gumbo. We all ate and talked til 6:30, and we were ready to begin.

The plan for the celebration was very simple. The main part was a chance for each of the Impalas to stand at the microphone and read something that they had written, roughly sequenced to follow the course of our journey. Then, there were some special thank-yous to our helpers, and at the end, some open-mic time for anyone who wanted to say a few words.

At the very start, the Impalas sang the Blackfish Paddle Song. The audience chairs were at the perimeter of the room in a few concentric rings, powwow style, with the big middle of the floor clear. The Impalas each got their paddles from the hallway and stood in the center, two sets of two rows, to emulate the Sunrise and Sunset crews. Daniel and Asia faced their crews with drums ready.

Eli made the introduction. "This is the Blackfish Paddle Song from the Jamestown S'Klallam Nation. Roger Fernandes taught it to us, and we have sung it at least a thousand times. He's right over there, hi Roger. But we want to sing it again, for you. In the song, you are going to hear us make a sound like this: *Whooo-Whoooo-Whooo*. It is the breath of *Klumachin*, the orca whale. When you hear that part, join in with us. You'll like it, it feels good. Thank you." Daniel and Asia started to play, and the Impalas paddled in place, and sang, and when it came around, the breath of the whale filled the room to the high ceiling.

I was sad to notice that some of our Impalas were not there. Gabe didn't make it, and a couple of others. That is what happens unless you can drive around to pick everyone up, which that evening we couldn't manage. But the Impalas left their crewmates' places empty, so that we remembered and honored them, paddling with us in the umiaks.

When the big thank-yous were done and people were sharing at the open-mic, Alyssa stepped up. I was standing in the back of the room beside the kitchen doors. I remember that I hoped that she would thank me, but she didn't. With tears on her face, she thanked Samantha for being there through everything that had happened. Which was right.

It was a warm and peaceful summer night when we had our hugs and our goodbyes, unfolding for a long time there on the sidewalk in the front of the school, surrounded by the lights of West Seattle, which were themselves surrounded by the darkness of the water of the Salish Sea that breathes in and out with the tides, holding the whole city in its arms.

~~~

That was the last time I saw any of the Impalas, but maybe one day I will see some of them again. Sometimes I wonder what our journey meant to them. I wonder what they remember. I wonder if any of them, like me, still have their paddles.

I did get to say my further goodbyes to my colleagues before I moved to North Carolina. I felt bad, saying farewell to Samantha. On the morning of the day that Alyssa was grounded and we drove to the beach to meet the umiaks, Samantha had given me her camera, asking me to take pictures of the Sunrise Crew as they approached the beach. I took the pictures, but when she asked me for her camera that night at the Carriers' place, I couldn't find it anywhere, and I never found it. Maybe I left it on a driftwood log at lunch, and the tide rose up and carried it away. I'm not sure if she forgave me.

As my family was packing up to move to North Carolina, Peter was packing up his apartment too, heading east for destinations unknown. I went by on the day he left. He sold me his cast-iron Jet table-saw for $35, and he honored me with a farewell smudge of sage, using a hawk's wing. I embraced him, and spoke a thank-you that seemed utterly inadequate, before we went our separate ways.

Pathfinder held a summer pow-wow, a few days before my departure. Some of the Elders surprised the teachers who were leaving the school that year with a farewell ceremony called the *Warrior's Dance*. It wasn't really a dance. We stood in the middle of the circle, and everyone in attendance stood and raised their palms, facing inward. In silence in the center of the circle, we each simply turned around once, slowly, step by step, with our arms outstretched downward, our palms facing outward to receive the blessing of the people. It was very powerful.

But most powerful of all was the moment when Ervanna stood at the microphone, and she told me that I was now her relative, that henceforth, she was claiming me as her brother. So on that day I gained a sister. I have not seen Ervanna in the time since, but I know that she completed graduate studies in indigenous education, and that she did research with the Maori people in New Zealand. She is a teacher and leader in her home community on the Warm Springs reservation in Oregon. Although we live and do our work 3,000 miles apart, I know that we are still paddling in the same umiak.

Deep Water

My long-time friend and brother Kevin Lee
Lopez writes me letters from cafes in St. Pete Beach,
scribed in black ballpoint pens on yellow pads. I carry his envelopes around with me, folded in half in my
back pocket, until I can find uninterrupted time to
read. About half the time I respond in kind with paper and envelopes, but half the time I resort to long
emails to which he replies curtly, encouraging me to
return to "the dignities of snail mail."

Kevin is Dakota from Crow Creek, South
Dakota. He is an *Inipi* leader and Sundancer, a liter-
ary critic, a middle-school teacher, and the director of
a new drama club comprised mostly of African-American sixth-grade girls from around Tampa Bay. A few
months ago, before I wrote this story, Kevin's latest
letter described the club's year-end performance of a

play that they had written themselves. In the course of the letter he described the foul language and general in-your-face unruliness of his young actors (an unruliness which dissolved into unengineerable brilliance under the lights of the performance itself). Pondering the next season of his drama club, he asked me, "Do you have any advice about sixth grade girls?"

To which I succumbed to the speed of the late-night keyboard. "I have no advice," I typed. "But I do have some stories to tell, about one sixth grade girl in particular." And I shared with him some of the stories I have shared with you here.

Kevin's email reply was predictably short, but it surprised me. Kevin wrote simply, *I will carry Alyssa to the Tree.* I knew that it meant that he would bring her in prayer to the Sundance Tree when he was in New Mexico for the ceremony the following week.

I am not on Facebook. Over the past seventeen years, I have returned to the Northwest once or twice, but the year of the Impalas has lived in a timeless bubble in my heart. My life here in the southern Appalachians has mingled with the lives of dozens and then hundreds of other children and families and classrooms, amid these forests of oak and rhododendron and ancient mountain rivers.

But last summer, after writing to Kevin and

reading his response, with all the memories of Alyssa bright in my heart, I decided to Google her, not really expecting anything to come up. I was on the screened-in porch at night, and all at once the floor beneath me dropped into deep water.

I saw many pictures of Alyssa, immediately recognizable. But they were on missing person sites. *The Charley Project*. *Black and Missing Foundation*. *Lost and Missing in Indian Country*. All the reports were consistent.

Seven years ago, when she was twenty-one, Alyssa disappeared. She was living with her three-year old daughter Nevaeh at her grandma Barbara's, and her mother was dying. Alyssa was last seen when she was approached on a Friday by a Caucasian man in a green pickup truck. The next day, a dispatcher received a 911 call from her cell phone and heard a woman's voice pleading for help, but the line went dead and could not be traced. She never came home to her daughter and her grandma. Her mother died three days later. Alyssa's partner, Nevaeh's father, said, "She is a devoted mother and very close to her own mom. Alyssa would never have abandoned our child."

I clicked through all the links, through the archives of all the subsequent years, my veins running cold, praying to see an update. There were posts

from her family and friends, never abandoning hope
of her safe return. But there were no updates. No
trace of Alyssa has yet been found.

~~~

Is there anyone among us
who has not closed the curtains, silenced the phone,
and wandered around the house, blind with grief?
Who has not moved across days that run together,
washing the dishes or folding the clothes
when that wave rises up?
The water fills the boat
and the boat goes down,
and down again.
For a time we seem to surface,
we think that we see the sky,
but then another wave is upon us,
the boat goes down again,
and there is no bottom.

~~~

Brown Leaves Falling in April

When my family moved into our house in Asheville, there was a giant tulip poplar tree not far from the back door. It was nearly a hundred feet tall, and at certain times in summer its leaves filled with fireflies, all the way to the top.

In April of 2007, a record-breaking cold snap stalled in the North Carolina mountains for four days. The temperature at night dropped to fifteen degrees and did not get above freezing in the day. Our tulip tree had just leafed out, with hundreds of thousands of tender bright green leaves, each the size of my hand. By dawn on the third day of the cold, all of the leaves on the tree were brown, and that morning they started to fall. I picked them up from the patio and held them in my hands.

Something about the falling of the dead leaves

in April was crushing to my heart. On that Sunday morning I wrapped my arms around the trunk of the old tree. My arms only reached halfway around, and my chest was pressed against the bark. I looked up into the branches of brown leaves and wept, and I asked the tree, "What are you going to do? Are you going to die?"

The tulip tree was bare for four weeks, but in the middle of May, it somehow pushed out a whole second set of leaves, not quite as large as the first, but enough to make its food from the sun through the summer and the fall. And from that time forward, the tulip trees and I have been in relationship.

The next summer, I was on a camping trip with several other families. It was a warm early evening and I was supposed to be helping, but I felt a fever coming on like a freight train. I retreated to my tent and was shivering in my sleeping bag as my temperature rose. I knew it was something like the flu and that it would have a run of several days or a week. I looked up through the transparent plastic skylight in the rainfly, and saw that there was a giant old tulip poplar right above the tent, its leaves lit up in the evening sun. I felt like I was seeing an old friend, and I greeted the tree and said that I was happy to be sleeping under its branches. Then I fell into dreamtime.

Over the course of that whole night, even in my sleep, I was aware of the presence of the big tree. After a while, according to the slow and steady way of the standing ones, I felt the tulip tree begin drawing the sickness out of my body and down into its roots beneath the ground under my tent. All night long, I could feel the pull of that energy into the earth, and I could feel my illness leaving me. When a high fever drops I always sweat, but that night I stayed cool and dry in my sleeping bag. When the sky grew light in the morning, I rose, and I was whole again and full of energy, as if the sickness itself had been a dream.

The next year, my wife Rhett and I noticed that the tulip tree outside our back door had a rotten area at the base of its trunk. Rhett was concerned about it and asked me to see what an expert would say. One winter day I asked my friend Dave Prophet, who sometimes brings me firewood. Dave is in his 70s, strong of body from hand-splitting countless cords of hardwood with a maul. When we work together, he pauses now and then to proclaim quotes from the Acts of the Apostles. He probed the rotten area at the base of the tree for a while with his fingers.

"Doesn't look good."

"So could that tree come down in the wind?" I asked.

"Oh yes. If an east wind caught it in full sail, it could fall on the house."

"And then?"

"Forget the upstairs. That tree wouldn't stop falling until it bounced on your kitchen floor."

So I tried to come to terms with the idea of having someone take down that tree. For a couple of months, feeling safe in the knowledge that the tree was bare and wouldn't catch the wind, I couldn't bring myself to do anything. Then one early spring night, I was lying on my back up on the roof of the kitchen, which I like to do. I looked up into the branches of the tree, which were a month from leafing out. I stayed there for a long time, and I shared everything with the tree, all the thoughts that were in my heart. And the tree responded.

It is a funny thing, trying to explain how animals or trees can communicate specific information to people. I was reminded of the Makah hunters' story that the whale had told them the night before the hunt when and where it would rise in the morning. It is not as though non-human beings use our language. They speak wordlessly, directly to our minds and hearts. Yet the communication can be very clear and very specific, and then we can retrieve it and translate it into words in our minds.

The tulip poplar tree told me that night that it was ready to go, that it was truly okay for us to take it down, but that there was a condition. The tree told me that it wanted its wood to be used for a ceremonial fire.

This struck me as odd, because tulip wood is not usually used for burning. No one here uses it in their wood-stoves because it does not approach the heat output of locust or hickory. People avoid it for outdoor fires too, because it pops and sparks. But the message was clear, and I did not hesitate. I wanted to take the tree down before it leafed out, so I hired a local tree crew for the next week. A man climbed the tree with spikes and ropes and took it down with his chainsaw, piece by piece. His one partner lowered the massive logs to the ground with ropes. I cut the logs up with a chainsaw and split them myself, and filled my woodshed with several cords of the pale yellow-gray smooth-grained fragrant tulip wood to dry. And as easily and deeply as I can grieve when loved ones pass, I noticed that I was not grieving for the tree at all. I realized it was because the tree was still guiding its destiny. This knowledge was not in my head, but in my heart.

On the Transformation of Suffering

But grief fell soon enough, as it can, like a great blade. I was teaching third grade at a remarkable place called Evergreen Community Charter School, in east Asheville. The following winter, over the holiday break, four students at our school lost parents, suddenly and tragically. A brother and sister's father was killed in a car accident on an icy highway. Another brother and sister lost both of their parents in a terrible case of domestic violence, a murder-suicide that involved a stand-off with the police, so it was in the news for all to see.

The staff of our school convened early before the end of the break to talk about how to handle all this with our students. The children who had lost both parents were taken in by their aunt and uncle. All four students would be coming back to school, so that something could remain normal and stable in their lives. Our staff met with a psychologist and came up with a plan of support for the grieving children, and also a plan for how to talk about the tragedies with their classmates.

It was during one of these conversations that I felt a tug on my heart from the tulip tree, and I shared the thought of having a simple, inclusive ceremonial fire, to help our community move through this together. My colleagues were open to the idea. The kids would return on Tuesday, and we would have the fire on Friday. And so my task was to figure out how it would go.

The plan and the pattern for the ceremony came incrementally over the course of that first week of school. On Thursday, we prepared a fire ring in the center of our school athletic field. We made a large circle of stones and filled them with rock screenings to protect the grass. I brought the tulip poplar wood ~ all of it ~ to school and we made a wall of firewood at the edge of the field. During the week, I had explained the plan for the ceremony to the four students who had lost their parents, and had asked each of them if they would be willing to be the fire-lighters, just the four of them, early on Friday. They all said yes.

On that cold January morning, a teacher or assistant-teacher walked each of the students up to the field. There was a kindergarten boy, a second grade girl, a fourth grade girl, and a seventh grade boy. The wood was arranged with eight logs in a simple pattern, with four places around it for lighting. There were four candles ready in jars, each with a lighting stick. We did not place an air of formality over any of this. There was a natural sense of respect, but we did not hesitate to be relaxed and even to joke around a little bit. After a minute or two of silence, the children lit the fire at the same time.

I had placed a bowl full of cornmeal at the edge of the fire. Cornmeal is sometimes used in American Indian ceremonial contexts, but in our case it was simply an inclusive invitation, so that if anyone at the fire wanted to silently send out *a good thought, a thank-you, or a request for help,* sprinkling a pinch of cornmeal in the fire was a way to do that. This is a tradition that I have used on school campouts many times. I think of it as a mindfulness practice, and in my experience, people of any religious or prayer tradition, or none at all, embrace and enjoy it. The four students sat with the fire for a few minutes. They each sprinkled a pinch of cornmeal in the flames, and then they went back inside to join their classes.

For the school day, I served as fire-keeper, but I had met with many of our teachers and staff the day before to share about fire-keeping, because the teachers had volunteered for shifts, from two to six hours long. The fire the children started would be kept going through the weekend, for three days and three nights. There would always be a fire-keeper awake. For the next seventy-two hours, the fire was available day-and-night for anyone in our community to come and sit, have some reflective time, talk respectfully or sit in silence, and leave whenever they wanted to go.

Around the fire we had put a circle of benches, and inside the benches were blankets on the ground. Over the course of that first day, each teacher in the school brought his or her class out to the fire as a group, for thirty minutes or so. They sat in a circle on the benches and passed the talking stick, once around. Nobody had to say anything, but whoever had any words they wanted to share was invited to do so. The ceremony became a place where children could speak and grieve their own losses ~ the passing of pets, of grandparents ~ as well as to speak to the intense losses of their four classmates.

It was a blessing to hold space for this. The talking circles were beautiful, both in the words shared and the silences shared. Although there were some differences in the kinds of words spoken among the five-year-olds and the fourteen-year-olds, the underlying energy of the circles around the fire was the same: deep, energetic, unforced and beautiful. The students sprinkled cornmeal silently into the flames before departing.

We had wanted to include the parents in our community, who had also been deeply affected by the events during the holiday break, so we decided to invite everyone to the fire at the end of the school day on Friday. Because we knew that there would be a lot of people - it turned out to be well over 500 - I knew that we needed to do something different. A story came to me to share. It began with my memory of a story that I had heard the great storyteller Michael Meade tell on a recording. I didn't remember it perfectly, and new parts came to me to add. I loved Michael's story because it also had a song, which he taught to his listeners, and I wanted everyone on Friday to have a chance to sing. Singing is the best way to remember to breathe.

I have since found Michael Meade's telling of the original. One needs to use great care with sacred stories, and I hope and trust that my changes and additions are okay. After our whole ceremony was over, I wrote the new old story down.

That afternoon we gathered in concentric circles around the fire the children had started. We had a speaker and a cordless microphone, and my dear friend, our music teacher Sue Ford, played a djembe to accompany me as I spoke. This is the story I told on that day.

Ka-ne-ro

*A story from indigenous South America,
reinterpreted by Chris Weaver, with gratitude to:
Michael Meade and all the story-keepers,
the teachings of Ho'oponopono,
the tulip poplar tree,
and the four fire-lighters.*

Once upon a time there was a village.
It was summer, and all the people
were out in the sun in the forest
doing the things they do in summer,
gathering food and playing games
and tracking animals and weaving mats,
when all at once a great wind arose
and a great darkness, followed by
a tremendous rain the likes of which
no one had ever seen before.
The rain was like being underneath a waterfall.
The people of the village, spread out as they were
across the land, scrambled for any shelter

111

the could find ~ a cave, a big fallen tree trunk ~
where they huddled in small groups
and listened to the huge noise of the wind and water.
The storm went on all day and all night.
It was an endless time out of time.

When at last the rain and wind stopped
and sunlight fell again across the forest,
the people came out from their shelters
to find one another, and they found themselves
gathered on the shore of a great river
where there had been no river ever before.
The water had carried the familiar land away,
it had pushed the whole continent apart,
and this vast river was flowing there in the West.
The people on the riverbank realized
that many of their people were not with them,
many of their people were on the other side
of this river. They could not see the other bank,
it was far away and covered in a thick cloud.
And everyone was separated
from somebody, every person discovered suddenly
these absences in their heart: friends were separated
from friends, mothers were separated
from their children, children were separated
from their fathers, grandmothers were separated
from their grandchildren.

After a while some of the men said,
We have to paddle over there to see
how our relatives are doing, to see that they
are alright. And so they fashioned a canoe.
They made it from the hardest tree of the forest
and they carried it to the edge of the water
and they set that canoe into the river.
But when that canoe touched the water
it began to melt, and it melted away, as though
it had been made of soft mud by the hands
of a child. And the people knew in that moment
that this is not a river that human beings
have the ability to cross.
And the people sat there on the bank of the river,
too shocked even to weep, and a deep silence
fell over them.

It happened that a small bird flew out of the forest
and circled in the sky up above the people.
Even as they had lost their voices,
the bird also did not have a song.
After a while the bird broke its circle and flew
straight across the flowing water of the river
until he disappeared into the cloud
that shrouded the other side.

After a long time, a young girl pointed,
and the children all pointed, and the fathers
and mothers and grandfathers and grandmothers
all pointed, because that little bird had emerged
from the cloud and was flying across the water
toward them. It circled again above them.
This time the bird had a song!
But the sound of his song was like the sound
of people weeping and crying,
and in the sound of this weeping the people heard
the voices of their loved ones across the river.
But the silence had been broken at last,
and someone spoke up to say, *Who is this bird*
who speaks with the voices of our relatives?

The little girl who had pointed spoke up and said,
I know this bird! This bird is named Ka-ne-ro.
And the people spoke his name: *Ka-ne-ro.*
All at once, the people began to weep themselves,
they cried and cried, and as they wept they noticed
that Kanero had become silent, he was flying
in a circle above their heads and he was listening
to their crying. And a moment later,
Zoom!
that Ka-ne-ro flew straight off to the West
across that river, and disappeared into that cloud.

The people watched him disappear and they said,
We want that Ka-ne-ro to come back!
Maybe if we build a fire he will see it!
So the people built a fire there on the river bank
and they gathered there around that fire,
waiting.

There he is! someone said,
and Ka-ne-ro flew out of that cloud,
and saw that fire, and came right over the heads
of the people and flew around in circles. Once again,
that Ka-ne-ro was singing, and once again
the people heard the voices of their relatives,
but this time, the voices were saying,
I'm sorry, I'm sorry, I am so sorry….
The people began to weep again, thinking
about their fathers and grandmothers and children
across the river, and they themselves began to say,
Yes, I am so sorry…
I am sorry that I did not listen to you,
I am sorry that I was angry with you,
I am sorry that this storm came so suddenly,
I am sorry I did not hold you in my arms,
I am sorry that I did not have a chance
to say goodbye.

That Ka-ne-ro had been listening to all this, and
Zoom!
off he flew to the West across that river.
Quietly weeping there, the people waited.

After a while, Ka-ne-ro came back.
He flew around in circles above the fire,
above the upturned faces of the people, singing.
This time the people heard their relatives saying,
Please forgive me...
Many times in many ways, *Please forgive me,*
and eagerly the people listened to all of it,
and they began to say *Yes! Of course,*
of course I forgive you! And some of them
were even laughing.

Then they raised their faces to the sky
and began to say, *But will **you** please forgive **me**?*
A son to his mother: *Please forgive me*
for the time I left the gate open
and all the goats got out!
A father to his teenage daughter:
Please forgive me for the time I wouldn't
let you see that boyfriend of yours I didn't like,
because I know you saw him anyway,
and he turned out to be okay after all.
All this *Please forgive me* floated up

116

to the magical listening ears of Ka-ne-ro, and
Zoom!
off that bird flew across that river and into that cloud.
Quiet and thoughtful, the people waited.

Ka-ne-ro came back again.
This time the little bird's voice was singing,
Thank you!
And the people listened to many many *Thank yous*
and they began to also say,
Thank you,
Thank you for all the love you shared,
thank you for your smile,
thank you for your hard work when no one was looking,
thank you for never giving up on me,
thank you for the bright shining light
that you were in my life,
when we were together.

And the people were weeping again, but this time
they were smiling through their tears.
Ka-ne-ro listened for a long time, and then
Zoom!
he flew into the West and disappeared again.

Ka-ne-ro came back again, one more time.
It would be the last time the people
would ever see Ka-ne-ro with their human eyes.
The people listened to his voice as he flew
in long slow circles above the fire. His voice sang,
I love you. I love you. I love you.
And the people said, *Yes,*
I love you, I love you,
and all these *I love you*s floated up to Ka-ne-ro.
But when all those *I love you*s entered his ears
and entered his little-bird heart,
something happened to Ka-ne-ro.
Ka-ne-ro *evolved.*
Kind of like a *Pokemon.*
Ka-ne-ro evolved, and got some more superpowers.
(And you know, this is what happens to us
when our hearts get so full of *I love you,*
we get so full of *I love you* that we evolve,
we are still ourselves but we notice
that we have some new superpowers.)
Ka-ne-ro's new superpowers were
that he no longer needed to use his voice to sing,
and he no longer needed to use his wings to fly.
That Ka-ne-ro gained the power to carry
each and every message directly into the heart
of the person it was intended for.
Neither space nor time was an obstacle to Ka-ne-ro.

He was faster than the speed of light, so that
the moment a message of love arose in the heart
of any of those people in that village, Ka-ne-ro
delivered that message exactly where it needed to go,
instantly.

So the people of that village
made a song for Ka-ne-ro,
and I am going to teach you that song.
The words are simple,
and the translation of this song is,
Ka-ne-ro, we need you, please come help us out.
And the second verse means,
Ka-ne-ro, thank you.
Try it, repeating after me:

Ka-ne-ro, E-te e-te,
Ka-ne-ro, E-te e-te,
Ka-ne-ro, E-te e-te,
Ka-ne-ro, E-te e-te.

Ka-ne-ro, No-ma no-ma,
Ka-ne-ro, No-ma no-ma,
Ka-ne-ro, No-ma no-ma,
Ka-ne-ro, No-ma no-ma.

That was really good. So now we will sing this song by the fire, because we need some help today from Ka-ne-ro, we are sending out a lot of messages on this day. So I invite you to sing with me, a few times through, and when we finish we will be quiet for a while, we will sit here together for a while, and listen.

The silence following the song was like a strong deep current of listening. Carrying the 500 people, it flowed for a long time, and I did not want it to stop.

I had in my hand a bell that my students call the Meeting Bell, which is actually a large upside-down heavy steel army-surplus cooking bowl with a hole drilled in the top, a rope to suspend it, and a thick poplar-wood dowel to ring it with. The silence continued until a young boy's voice piped up brightly to the crowd:

"So what's next?"

Laughter rippled around. It was the youngest of our fire-lighters, sitting on his kindergarten teacher Heather's lap. I tiptoed between the kids on the blankets over to him, gave him the stick, and held out the upside-down bowl by its rope. He whacked it hard, and it rang. The people applauded and laughed and stood up, and the crowd began to drift back to the school building to go home for the weekend.

Wildfire

Over the course of the next three days, many parents visited the fire, sometimes with their kids, sometimes on their own. They came by day and by night. They brought food for the teacher fire-keepers. No one knows all the words that were shared quietly there. We were blessed with clear weather, but it was January, and the night-time fire-keepers wrapped heavy blankets around their backs. Whenever the fire burned down to the point where the last yellow flame disappeared in the pile of glowing coals, the fire-keeper would bring wood over from the pile and re-build the eight-log pattern, and the flames would leap to life again. There was a constant staccato crackle of the popping tulip wood, and the all the blankets had dozens of small holes burned into them from the sparks.

One other thing happened in that ceremony that bears recounting.

It was 2:00am on Saturday night, the middle night of the ceremony. The fire-keeper was the school's director of admissions, Robin. Her shift was from midnight to 6am, and she was alone with the fire.

As she sat there, all at once Robin's whole body was filled with a very intense and disruptive force of energy. It was an energy of unspeakable and almost unbearable rage. Robin felt the energy in her body and the rage surging in her heart, but she knew that the emotions were not her own.

When the energy continued on and on, Robin needed help. She immediately thought of her friend Jewel, a Christian missionary on the Kiowa reservation in Oklahoma, and called her on her cell phone. Jewel answered the late-night call and Robin told her what was going on. Having her friend's voice on the phone helped her to stay calm. Her friend kept listening for a long time as Robin described what was happening with the energy in her body, and Jewel held her in prayer. After a long time the wildfire of rage gave way to an unfathomably deep river of sadness, and the tears flowed from Robin's eyes. Little by little, the sadness too began to subside, until Robin felt as though she was sitting on a soft dry sand beach. With her friend Jewel still on the line,

Robin found herself on her blanket by the fire under the winter stars, feeling like herself again.

When I relieved her in the darkness at 6am to take the Sunday morning shift, she told me about her experience. Robin had no doubt about what had happened. She knew that she had been visited by someone she knew, the children's mother who had been killed two weeks before. Robin knew that something about her own presence there with the fire had provided an invitation, a chance for the mother's spirit to rage, and to grieve, and to let go, so that she could continue on her journey.

Dedication

The British scholar and mystic Peter Kingsley reminds us that the word for *wisdom* in ancient Greek is *Alethia,* which translates literally as *not forgetting.* Alethia's opposite is *Lethe,* the river of forgetfulness and oblivion, one of the five rivers of the underworld. Kingsley says that in our time, the River Lethe is in flood, and it is a flood of biblical proportions. Kingsley urges Westerners to *remember,* not by appropriating the traditions of other cultures, but by unearthing the lost teachings in the pre-Socratic roots of Western civilization. There we can find long-forgotten *operating instructions,* sacred guidance to transform us beyond the destructive ignorance of our modern culture, which has ravaged the earth.

The Native author, artist, musician and teacher Martin Prechtel says that our loved ones who have died travel safely to the other side in a canoe borne on the warm salty water of our tears. So perhaps there is remembering to be done about how to grieve together, how to transform our suffering. Perhaps when the rights and traditions of indigenous people are fully honored and protected, then more of these gifts can be shared.

It also seems that old and new need one another. New forms are unrooted without the wisdom of the old. Yet old forms are limited without a transforming infusion of the new. Even as the pathologically forgetful aspects of modern culture have flooded the earth, human consciousness has also evolved to a moment of acute creative potential, of new birth.

In the teachings of *A Course in Miracles* there is a startling reinterpretation of the idea of memory. Our memories of the past do nothing but perpetuate the illusions of the past. But the human capacity to remember can be used differently. With the right Guide, it is possible, and necessary, and liberating, to remember not the past, but to *remember the present*. We can remember the present moment in all its fullness, and this is the same as remembering God. It is the only use of memory that is trustworthy.

This has become how I think about ceremony. Ceremony is *holding space to remember the present, together.* Forgiveness and healing and the release of our ancestors are some of the fruits of ceremony like this.

And so there are vessels afloat on the waters of oblivion. There are vessels being made, being imagined, being remembered. Their movement is simple and graceful and ancient, but their forms are also new. Among their paddles are the paddle of *story*, and the paddle of *ceremony*. They are Canoes, and they have a heart. And the heart of the Canoe knows where it is going.

~~~

Back in June, when I learned of Alyssa's disappearance, I knew that I needed a ceremony, and that I needed to share it with others. But nobody near me had ever heard her name, or argued with her, or beheld her standing her ground like a tigress on the beach. So the ceremony I made is the writing of this book. With gratitude, I share the story with you. And with love, I dedicate it to her.

The Heart of the Canoe

November 29, 2016

Dedicated to

Alyssa Angelique McLemore,

the world's child.

Epilogue

I bit the bullet and got on Facebook, and Alyssa's grandma Barbara became my first *friend*. I asked her if she thought it was okay for me to write to Alyssa's daughter Nevaeh, to share some stories about her mom. Barbara replied,

> She would love that. I am taking her to her first Sundance. She will walk on the same Sacred ground as her Mother. It was her idea...she is almost 11. She is so much like Alyssa that people have deja vu seeing us together. Her temperament is more like her Dad...she is extremely well behaved and quiet and helpful. My first Great-grandchild. Hope that things are going well with you.

So it was time to write a letter. I decided to send it *snail-mail*.

~~~

This story is finished. But I wrote above that no true story has a beginning or an end. In this spirit, I have two postscripts to share.

First. Over time, Barbara shared with me that the Medicine People believe that Alyssa is still alive. In my experience, they know. If her disappearance was an isolated act of violence, this would be impossible. But Alyssa may instead be a victim of organized human trafficking, an underworld that is international in scope. It has been suggested that she may be in the Middle East. Any readers with information to share are invited to contact alyssa@spring-branchpress.org.

The second postscript is about the Canoe Nations. The cultural revival has grown in the past seventeen years. This summer, in 2016, the Nisqually Nation on the southern Salish Sea hosted the ceremonial paddle, around the theme, *Don't Forget the Water*. On July 30th, more than 100 canoes arrived on Nisqually beaches from their long journeys. For the first time, a canoe joined from the East Coast Sister Algonquin tribes, Wampanoag, Nipmuc, Shinnecock and Montauk, led by Butterfly Woman. All the canoes were greeted by more than 10,000 people, for a week of ceremony and celebration.

And, five weeks later, Canoe Families from the Tlingit, Haida, Warm Springs, Puyallup, Quinault,

Chehalis, Colville, Nisqually, Muckleshoot, Coeur D'Alene, and other northwest Nations answered the call and towed their dugouts across the continental divide to Standing Rock in North Dakota. To the sound of their songs and drums, the paddlers guided the cedar canoes from Bismarck down the Missouri River and up the Cannonball River to Sacred Stone Camp. They asked permission to land in the traditional way, and were welcomed by their Oceti Sakowin hosts to join in the stand of the great tree to protect the water of the high plains, along with 300 other indigenous Nations in a gathering unlike any seen before in history.

Mni Wiconi.

The story continues.

May we remember the present, together, with gratitude.

All proceeds from the sale of this book go to Alyssa's family,
to be shared in her honor.

To join an online conversation about *The Heart of the Canoe*,
visit theheartofthecanoe.org.

About the Author

Chris Weaver lives with his wife Rhett Hudson in Asheville, North Carolina. They have two sons: Aidan, a filmmaker, and Noah, a musician. Chris has taught in elementary school classrooms for 20 years, in North Carolina, Washington, and Colorado. He designed and directed camp-based programs for teenagers in foster care from across North Carolina, and taught summer middle-school with the Colorado Migrant Education Program. In 2014-15 he served as North Carolina Charter School Teacher of the Year. Chris is the author of *Living School Design & Practice* (to be published early in 2017), which shares a comprehensive design for a new kind of school. Beginning in June of 2017, the *Living Schools Collaborative* will offer workshops and mentoring in year-long cohorts for people interested in starting new schools. Information is available at **living-schools.org**.

About the Artist

Paula M. Nelson was born and raised on the Qualla
Boundary in North Carolina as a enrolled tribal member
of the Eastern Band of Cherokee Indians, also known as
the Anikituwahgi. She lives in the Kolanvyi Community
and is a multi-media artist, singer, songwriter, poet, per-
former, and living history educator, specializing in time
periods from Archaic, Mississippian, Historic and Modern. Paula has worked for many Cherokee cultural insti-
tutions, educational organizations throughout the country and abroad, and Native American events as an inter-
preter of her Native culture in historical context. She is
known for her powerfully educational audience-inclusive
performances. Paula currently works from her home
studio in her community, and spends her time writing
poetry and songs, working in mixed media, and perform-
ing when called upon.

Made in the USA
San Bernardino, CA
16 January 2017